£££

HOW TO BECOME A WOMAN OF SUBSTANCE

Anthea Masey

PIATKUS

First published in Great Britain
in 1987 by
Judy Piatkus (Publishers) Limited,
5 Windmill Street, London W1

British Library Cataloguing in Publication Data
Masey, Anthea
How to become a woman of substance.
1. Women——Finance, Personal
I. Title
332.024'042 HG179

ISBN 0–86188–666–6
ISBN 0–86188–671–2 Pbk

Phototypeset in 10½/12pt Linotron 202 Sabon
Printed and bound in Great Britain at
The Bath Press, Avon

£££

Contents

£££

Introduction

Money is the last frontier. Women may be out there fighting for their place next to men in the civil service and the professions. In business they may be slowly clambering up the management ladder. There may even be a few women entrepreneurs. But when it comes to handling our money, most of us have a hard job looking beyond the next hard-earned pay packet.

Why is it that women are good at looking after the pennies, but then discover there is no truth in the old adage that the pounds look after themselves?

The answer lies in our history and our culture. We know all about the housekeeping. We watched our mothers stretch their weekly allowance. We were there as she juggled the money so there was sometimes enough left over to buy material for a party dress or put a down-payment on a new piece of furniture.

Looking back it seems almost Dickensian. But it wasn't so very long ago that I remember the ritual of my father handing my mother her weekly allowance on a Friday morning, and the unseemly bargaining which went on when my mother wanted a rise.

Women may have held the purse strings, but the wallet with the pound notes stayed firmly under the control of the economically active male. The big financial decisions: like could you have that expensive long dress for the next school dance, could you have that new tape recorder, could you go on holiday with the school? All these were not in the gift of your mother. For an answer you had to wait until Father got home.

Most women of my generation remember the fear and trepidation with which we asked for some longed-for favour. Would he or wouldn't he say yes? The agonising wait for a final ruling. The unspoken burden of good behaviour which got thrown into the equation. Did we deserve this expensive treat?

Those of us who grew up in the kind of family where the father worked and brought home the money, and the mother stayed at home to look after the children, had the idea bred into us that all the good things in life came from men, but we somehow had to earn them.

There was also the notion that there was something intrinsically unladylike about money and that women shouldn't have to bother their pretty little heads with such sordid matters. The darkest secret between man and wife was not the extent of his infidelities, but the size of his pay packet.

Times have of course changed. Now most women work, and not just for pin money. We are ambitious and we want careers, not take-it-or-leave-it jobs. Our work is now as important to our well-being as our homes and families have always been. Nonetheless, the idea that we women aren't quite in control of the more important aspects of our finances is still buried deep in our psyche. We have seized control of the rest of our lives, isn't it time we took charge of our own financial destiny as well?

And let's stop pretending money isn't important to us. It is. It gives us freedom and independence. And it's not just a matter of being able to buy a new dress without having to ask a man for the money. It's much more fundamental than that. It's the freedom to walk away from a bad marriage, to take a career break while the children are small, to train for a new job, to take a trip round the world, to start our own business.

Novelist Virginia Woolf reckoned women failed to fulfil their potential for want of 'A Room of One's Own' – a space away from the clamour of the family where they could think, read and spend time on their own. But how many of today's women are economically trapped and fail to do themselves justice for want of money?

We start out at a natural disadvantage. Not only do we tend to earn less than men, but we take our family responsibilities much more seriously. Many of us opt to work part-time and those of us with children seem to prefer to take a career break while they are small. The woman who works 40 years for the same employer is a rare animal.

The broken pattern of our working lives may be a sign of sanity but it places us on the financial margin. As part-time workers, we are often denied full legal rights as employees. We may not be entitled to a whole range of State benefits if we fall ill or lose our jobs. And even if we work full-time we often lose out on fringe benefits, such as workplace pensions.

But when it comes to starting our own businesses necessity appears to be the mother of invention. Women commonly go into business after stopping work to have children. The evidence suggests that the entrepreneurial spirit hits women when they are still in their early 30s while men tend to wait until their late 30s before taking the plunge.

It's taking time, but there are signs that our financial aspirations are beginning to be taken seriously. The National Insurance system no longer penalises women for taking a career break to look after small children or elderly relatives. Improvements are being made to workplace pension schemes, and from 1988 we will be free to make our own pension arrangements. Employers are devising schemes which will give us back our old jobs after breaks of up to five years.

This book is designed to give you the confidence to take control of your money, to redress the balance of financial power in your family, and to start planning beyond your next pay cheque.

In Part One you will find the basics – how to budget, where to save, which type of mortgage to go for, where to buy cheap insurance, how to fill in your tax return and pay less tax, and how to avoid falling prey to the high pressure salesmen.

Part Two takes you further into areas where women traditionally fear to tread. To become a woman of substance you must get ready to storm that male bastion, the world where money makes money.

You have had all the fun of the Government share issues in British Telecom, British Gas and British Airways. Now experience the thrills and spills of investing for yourself on the Stock Exchange. Learn how to do it, and how to choose the winners. Find out if you have the right temperament for the fast-moving high-risk world of commodities and options.

Listen to what other women have to say about money. How they make it, how they handle it, how they invest it, and – most important of all – how they spend it. After all, spending it is what this careful husbandry is all about.

This book is not about squirrelling your money away just for the sake of having it for some proverbial rainy day. It's about getting the most out of your money. It's about making your money work for you. It's about setting objectives, so you are clear about what you want from your money. Above all it's about setting you free.

£££

PART ONE

£££

1
The balance sheet

Does your money burn a hole in your pocket? Are you always reaching for your credit cards come the middle of the month? Do you live in fear and dread of your bank manager? Do you have a sneaking feeling you aren't making the most of your money?

If you answer yes to any of the above you must be suffering from a case of financial unfitness. This book is designed to help you get in shape – and it won't be half as painful as working out in the gym.

WHERE DOES THE MONEY GO?

Do your hackles rise at the word budgeting? Does it bring forth images of the mean, the penny-pinching and the obsessional? If so, you are just like the rest of us, totally sane. Most of us prefer to think of ourselves as easy going, carefree, and fun-loving.

Life is just too short to record every casual cup of coffee, every newspaper, every chocolate bar you buy. That's not the way to financial fitness. If there was such a thing as financial anorexia, keeping a detailed note of everything you spend would be it. But there is no wriggling out of it, budgeting is the first step to financial fitness. However, I'm not going to ask you to keep a little notebook and log everything you spend down to the very last penny.

Instead, this budget is one you can do just once a year, and you can do it whenever you want. Perhaps, the best time psychologically is the New Year – that time of fresh starts and good resolutions, which seems to hit most of us as we come round from all that excess of Christmas spirit. Seize the moment while the feeling still lasts. But if you fail to catch it in time, wait until you get your tax return at the start of the new tax year, when your mind is focused on money anyway.

Your aim is to track down your income and where it went. You are preparing your own profit and loss account just as if you were a large public company. But if, like most people, your financial record keeping is at best the back of a drawer, at worst the waste paper bin, this may require some detective work.

Begin by gathering up as many payslips, dividend vouchers, bank and credit card statements, cheque books and bills as you can find. If there are big gaps, ask your bank manager to return all last year's cheques. They charge you for digging them out, but you won't get far without them.

The budget planner on pages 10–11 is comprehensive, so don't feel you have to follow it slavishly. Tailor it to meet your needs.

The thing about a budget is that it makes you think about where you are spending your money. This may be as important a function as actually getting the figures to come out to the last penny. And once you are convinced of the usefulness of the exercise, you will resolve to do it better next year. Even the most careless of record keepers can learn to fill in their cheque stubs with helpful information, and when the cheque book is finished toss them into a large envelope which can be brought out for this once-a-year exercise in financial totting up.

You may even invent your own short cuts – like using your bank credit card because you find their itemised accounts more helpful than a bank statement.

You should now have some idea of where your money is leaking out. Your aim is to stretch your money and make it perform miracles. Make yourself a draft budget for the coming year. Don't set yourself too many unrealistic targets. If you do you will lose faith in the whole exercise.

But if you love travelling, and all you managed last year was a two-week package tour to Majorca, pencil in something more exotic for the coming year, and transfer the money from one of the other categories. If you have a passion for designer clothes, but only managed one outfit last year, again see if you can find the money from somewhere else.

As you can see budgeting is not about penny-pinching. It's about robbing Peter to pay Paul, or using the money you waste to buy the things you really want.

The first lesson is don't ignore the essentials. We all have to eat, shelter, keep warm and pay our taxes. But it can be just as easy to fritter money on these as it is on life's little luxuries.

Food is likely to be a big item in your budget, with the average family spending around a fifth of their income on food[1]. If you are keeping the local corner store in business and yourself in ulcers with his frozen TV dinners, think about changing your habits and shopping more frequently at your nearest big supermarket. If you keep to a strict list, you will save pounds and your health too.

Are you paying too much for your heating? By spending money now, you may be able to cut your bills in the future.

Simple measures like insulating your loft and hot water tank, pay for themselves in less than two years[2].

Look at all your essential spending with the same critical eye. Are your rates too high? Could you profitably claim a reduction in your rateable value? Are you making too many long chatty phone calls at peak rates?

Now look at how you spend the rest of your money – what the economists like to call your discretionary spending. How much was planned and how much was spent on the spur of the moment and later regretted? This year decide to take control, and plan your spending. But leave some leeway. Life is no fun if there is no room for the occasional flight of fancy, and you are always looking over your shoulder at some oppressive budget. Don't make your budget into a straightjacket because with no room to manoeuvre, you will come to hate it.

BUDGET PLANNER

Income

	£
Income from employment:	
PAYE earnings (enter amount before tax)	——
Freelance and self-employed earnings (enter amount before tax)	——
Income from savings and investments:	
Income taxed at source – such as building societies, banks and company dividends (enter amount after tax)	——
Income not taxed at source – such as National Savings (enter amount before tax)	——
Any other income:	
Such as Child Benefit or other State benefits, alimony or child maintenance payments, income from investment property	——
Total income:	══

Expenditure

Essentials:	£		£
Food	——	Tax paid through PAYE	——
Mortgage or rent	——	National Insurance contributions	——
Rates and water rates	——	Pension contributions	——
Electricity	——	House maintenance	——
Gas	——	Buildings and house contents insurance	——
Other fuels	——	Travelling to work	——
Telephone	——	Child care	——
Tax paid on earnings and investment income not taxed at source	——		
Total essential expenditure:			══

BUDGET PLANNER

Expenditure

Non-Essentials:	£		£
Holidays	——	Life insurance	——
Drink and cigarettes	——	Regular savings plans	——
Entertaining and meals out	——	Personal Equity Plans	——
Presents	——	Other investments acquired	——
Car purchase	——	Clothes	——
Car maintenance	——	Newspapers, books and periodicals	——
Car insurance and road tax	——	TV rental and/or licence	——
Petrol	——	Hobbies	——
Tavel not already allowed for	——	Loan repayments	——
School fees	——	Bank and credit card interest	——
Home improvements	——	Children's pocket money	——
Housekeeping	——	Your own pocket money	——
Professional fees	——		
Trade union dues or subscriptions to professional bodies	——		

Total non-essential expenditure: ══

Total expenditure: ══

Excess (or otherwise) of income over expenditure: ══

Not everything you want can be encompassed within a year. The moment has now come for a little long-term planning. You want to buy a house, but need a deposit. You have a burning desire to spend a summer in some remote little village in Greece or go walking in the Himalayas. You are toying with the idea of setting up your own business.

Don't hope for some fairy godmother to wave her magic wand, the only person who can turn dreams into reality is you. And unless you hit the jackpot on the pools, the only way to do it is by saving some of your money. Aim to save between 10 and 15 per cent of what you earn. But if you are working on a really tight budget and this looks totally unrealistic try and find 5 per cent from somewhere.

HINTS TO HELP YOU BUDGET

○ Aim to pay no bank charges. The big high street banks offer free banking if you keep your bank account in the black. Unfortunately this does mean you have to keep a close eye on the state of your bank balance. Go into red by just a couple of pounds, and the banks charge you each time you write a cheque, make a standing order, or get a letter from your bank manager. And they don't just charge you when you are overdrawn, most of them carry on charging you for the whole of the three-month charging period.

○ If you are always running up bank charges by mistake because you find it difficult to keep track of what you are spending, think about opening a building society linked account. Choose between Alliance and Leicester's BankSave account linked with the Bank of Scotland, or Birmingham Midshires Mastercheque linked with the TSB. With these accounts your bank account is always kept in credit with automatic transfers from your building society account.

○ If you do need to overdraw, save bank charges by using as few cheques as possible. Use your bank credit card as much as possible. You then write just one cheque when your credit card payment is due. If you have several bills to pay at any one time, add them all together, make a cheque out to the bank, take it and the bills to the bank and let them sort it out.

○ Throw out any store credit cards. Store credit cards are just a way of getting you to buy more than you intend. Don't fall for it – most shops take other credit cards. The rate of interest is generally high – higher even than a bank credit card – and very few cards pay you interest if you have paid in more money than you have borrowed.

○ Throw out all charge cards. The principal charge cards are American Express and Diners Club. With charge cards, you get unlimited interest-free credit, but you must clear your account each month, and there is an annual charge. These cards are useful if you travel a lot and need to pay for airline tickets and hotels. If this is you, get your employer to pay the annual charge. Otherwise you don't need them.

○ Throw out all bank gold cards; they are an expensive luxury unless you need the automatic overdraft or want to impress your business contacts – see Chapter Fourteen. Gold cards work like charge cards: you must clear the account each month and there is an annual charge. You are unlikely to get one unless you earn at least £20,000 a year.

○ Keep your bank credit cards but use them sensibly. Bank credit cards are either the blue, gold and white Visa card, issued by Barclays Bank, the Bank of Scotland, and the Co-operative Bank, or the green, red and white Access card issued by Lloyds, Midland, National Westminster and the Royal Bank of Scotland. The cards are similar. Go shopping at the right time of the month, and you can get up to 56 days' free credit. And if you always clear your account each month, there is no other interest to pay. Don't use your bank credit cards to run up debts, the rate of interest is expensive – there are cheaper ways to borrow money.

○ Take out more than one bank credit card. You can apply to any bank for one and, with Access but not with Visa, it is worth trying to specify the payment date. This way you have several cards with different payment dates, and you choose which one to use to take advantage of the interest-free credit. Don't do this if you think a whole fist of credit cards will just encourage you to spend, spend, spend.

○ Investigate paying in instalments those bills which you usually pay in advance. Local authorities are legally required to offer ratepayers the chance of paying their rates by monthly instalments (usually 10), and they are not allowed to charge more for the service.

Most insurance companies now let you pay your house, contents and car insurance by monthly instalments. They often do charge more, but the advantage may still be yours if you can earn more by putting the money you have delayed handing over on deposit earning interest. It all depends on how much more they are charging.

○ Investigate operating budget accounts with your gas and electricity boards and spreading your bills equally over 12 monthly instalments. With gas and electricity bills which come in once a quarter, you get three months' free credit. On the face of it you are losing out if you pay once a month. However, if your bills fluctuate – perhaps they are larger in the winter when you turn the heat up – it's worth sitting down and doing the sums. Think about opening a budget account at the beginning of the winter. This spreads the cost of those heavy heating bills over into the summer.

○ Don't pay bills with savings stamps. You can buy telephone, TV licence and road tax savings stamps at most Post Offices and gas and electricity savings stamps at most gas and electricity board showrooms. Savings stamps are a bit of a con – they take your money and don't pay you any interest on it. If you are worried about having enough money to pay your bills when they come in, put something each month into a building society account specifically for that purpose. At least building societies pay interest.

HOW MUCH AM I WORTH?

If your budget is working you will want some way of measuring your growing affluence, how much you are actually worth. Just like any company you need your own personal balance sheet. Do this along with your budget and you will have a record of your hopefully growing fortunes.

How much are you worth? The calculation is a simple one. You are worth everything you own of value, less your debts.

Use the balance sheet on page 16 to find out how far you are up that yellow brick road.

If this exercise has done nothing but confirm your poverty, you are not alone. Becoming a woman of substance is going to be a hard struggle, as the statistics show. In 1984 the top 1 per cent owned 21 per cent of the nation's wealth, while the top 10 per cent owned 52 per cent.

Pension rights from both State and company pension schemes have a slight levelling effect. When these are included, the top 1 per cent's share of the nation's wealth falls to 12 per cent and the top 10 per cent's to 35 per cent[3].

Anyone who pays National Insurance contributions or who pays into their company pension scheme has pension rights. These only have a value at or near retirement when you have the right to start drawing a pension. To work out the value of your pension rights any earlier is a notoriously difficult task – one which needs the services of a trained actuary.

Even though your own balance sheet leaves out any pension rights, they may still be an important source of personal wealth, although for reasons you will discover later, women often get a very raw deal from pensions (see Chapter Nine).

WHAT AM I WORTH DEAD?

While you are busy setting yourself financial targets and priorities for the coming year you might consider just one last task. Try working out how much you would be worth if you died tomorrow.

BALANCE SHEET

Assets or belongings:

	£
Estimated market value of your house or flat	——
Personal belongings with a market value of at least £100	——
Jewellery	——
Collectables with a market value	——
Building society accounts	——
Bank deposit accounts	——
Government stocks	——
Company shares	——
Unit trusts	——
Surrender value of any life	——
insurance policies	——
Bullion coins	——
Total assets	═══

Debts:

Mortgage	——
Overdraft	——
Credit card debts	——
Outstanding hire purchase debts	——
Outstanding bank loans	——
Any other	——
Total debts:	═══

Assets less debts = total wealth

Only bother doing this if there are people who would suffer financially if you died, or you are so wealthy you should be thinking about ways of avoiding inheritance tax (see Chapter Seven). Even then you don't need to do it more than every couple of years or so.

If people are counting on your earning power, you probably need insurance. Choose the right insurance and it won't be a major expense. The first problem is knowing how much you need. There are two calculations: finding the size of the income gap and finding the size of the capital gap. You then plug them with insurance. See Chapter Seven.

The income gap is the difference between your family's income with you no longer there earning a living and how much they need to maintain their standard of living. Use the budget planner to work out the size of the deficit.

It's an exercise which is likely to leave you hopping mad and extremely disillusioned with State and workplace pension schemes and contracts of employment. These are still designed for men with little regard for the contribution that women now make to the family budget.

In fact many families are better off if the husband dies rather than the wife. When the husband dies his wife gets one of a range of state widow's pensions if she is over 40 or there are children, and a pension from his workplace scheme.

If the wife dies, there is no State pension for her widower. Nor is there much joy from workplace pension schemes. Few of these offer their women employees an automatic widowers' pension, even though they will be required to do so from 1988.

Now is the time to look for your pension scheme booklet and discover if your family can expect an income from your workplace pension scheme, and how much it is likely to be.

Your family can also get One-Parent Benefit in addition to Child Benefit. The supplement is the same whether there is one child or six. In the 1987/88 tax year it came to £4.70 a week.

Now you have some idea of how much money your family would have coming in if you fell under the proverbial bus. The next task is to work out how much they would spend. The mortgage, rates and most of the bills stay the same whether or not you are there. But there would be a reduction in the food and clothing bills, and in the amounts spent on your hobbies.

But there will be other major expenses. If you look after small children as well as work, the family needs to pay for the children to be looked after if you are no longer there. And they may need some help with the housework. One major insurance company, the Legal and General, reckons that it costs £370 a week to replace the housekeeping and child care services of a stay-at-home wife.

Your family may be saddled with extra expenditure if they have come to rely on perks from your job. So add something if, for example, your firm picks up the tab for your petrol.

You can now calculate the size of the income gap which would hit your family if you were no longer around to bring in a wage packet.

Next, you need to know the size of the capital gap. The purpose of this exercise is to find out whether there is enough readily available money to repay all your debts, and replace any assets which went with your job.

If you are mortgaged up to the hilt and have borrowed to buy most of what you own, you could be leaving your family with a visit from the bailiff.

Start by taking another look at the booklet which goes with your workplace pension scheme. Many schemes now pay out a lump sum if you die before reaching retirement age. And these payments are made regardless of sex and whether or not you have dependants. The usual sum is between two and two-and-a-half times your annual salary.

Make sure you understand your life insurance policies. If you have life insurance savings plans the sum you get if you die early may be different (it's often higher) than the cash-in value. You may have other life insurance policies which only have a value if you die. If you have a loan with your bank or a finance company, check the small print. Some loans give you automatic life insurance to cover the cost of repaying the loan if you die before you finish paying it off. Check all these and remember to enter them on the asset side of your balance sheet.

Your family will also need to replace assets which went with your job. If you have an office car, you need to make sure they have enough money to replace it with. So enter the amount which is needed to buy a new car as a debt on your balance sheet. If your family could end up paying inheritance tax, the estimated amount is also entered as a debt.

You now have the measure of how much your family would inherit and if there is enough money to repay your debts. If your figures throw up a capital gap, you will need to think about taking out more life insurance. For the best sorts of policy, follow the advice in Chapter Seven.

[1] *Social Trends 17* 1987 Edition, table 6.11.
[2] *Which?* October 1986.
[3] Inland Revenue.

£££

2
Small beginnings

Beware the bearer of gifts. Treat anyone who knocks on your door, rings you up over the telephone, or stops you in the street, with enormous suspicion. If they call themselves a financial adviser, or tax consultant, slam the door, put down the phone or walk away. They are likely to be nothing of the sort. They are probably commission-hungry life insurance salesmen. Or worse. They could be pushing shares in some small, obscure, overseas company which no one has ever heard of, or a commodity scheme guaranteed to double your money overnight. Don't let the confidence tricksters part you from your money.

Not everyone needs life insurance, and those that do certainly don't need to buy it from a high-pressure salesman who is in the habit of selling high-cost policies to the wrong people. And you certainly don't need to put your hard-earned cash into some hair-brained investment scheme. It might sound tempting, but the only pocket you will be lining is the salesman's.

When it comes to the hard sell, it could be that our supposed lack of financial acumen stands us in good stead. I know men who are plagued by unsolicited telephone calls from so-called 'financial advisers'. I've watched the clip-board merchants quarry their prey with obvious instructions to only approach presentable young men under the age of 30 and to leave the women alone.

Women are not yet seen as an easy marketing target for life

insurance. May that last as long as it takes us to learn the uses and abuses of life insurance so that when we do get cornered by one of those zealous salesmen we have the knowledge to see through his sales spiel.

Over the last 10 years, several insurance brokers and life insurance companies have had a go at women. They have come up with complicated packages designed to allow for the fact that women's working lives are rarely continuous. But as this is not really a problem if you are buying the right kind of life insurance, most of these packages are nothing short of an overpriced marketing gimmick. So particularly avoid any life insurance policies marked 'for women only', and don't be taken in by the pretty pictures in the brochure.

The trouble with life insurance, and it's a problem that few insurance salesmen are willing to spend time explaining, is that it is really two different things. It is:

- A useful and often cheap way of making sure your dependants don't suffer financially if you die prematurely.

- A way of saving money.

The first is worth having; the second, unless it is linked to a mortgage, is usually a waste of money. And yet, because the salesman earns a bigger commission cheque when he sells a savings-type policy than when he sells a simple life protection policy, a lot of people are missing out on the best life insurance deals. See Chapter Seven.

Having disposed of the high-pressure insurance salesman, you are now free to think about the best places to save your money.

The first and only rule when you start saving is keep it simple. Get to know what National Savings, the building societies and the banks offer. With everyone tripping over themselves in the fight to get their hands on your savings, the choice even among these relatively staid institutions is now bewilderingly wide. Compared with the fortunes being made on the Stock Exchange, they may appear unadventurous. But they do have the advantage of being predictable and safe. And they won't cause you any sleepless nights. These days they even offer a real rate of return too.

The 1970s and early 1980s were not a good time for small savers. It was an uphill struggle protecting your savings from the ravages of inflation. Now inflation is down in single figures this is no longer a problem. To earn a real rate of return, your savings must grow faster than the rate of inflation. For example, if inflation is 5 per cent and your savings are earning 8 per cent interest, your real rate of return is 3 per cent.

Having mastered the intricacies of the various schemes on offer from National Savings, the building societies and banks, you can start thinking about a first dabble on the stock market through a unit trust regular savings scheme, or a Personal Equity Plan.

It's hard work fighting your way through the savings jungle. You will get bogged down unless you know where you are going and have clearly defined your aims. Ask yourself the following questions:

- Why am I saving and how long for?
- Will I be tempted to dip into the money before I reach my goal?
- What's my tax position?

WHY AM I SAVING AND HOW LONG FOR?

EMERGENCY FUND

You should aim to have an emergency fund – money which you can get your hands on at short notice, if your roof blows off or your car breaks down and needs expensive repairs. Two months' after-tax salary is a good figure to aim for. Don't leave this kind of money hanging around in your bank current account, earning money for the bank and not for you. Put it where it earns interest, and where you can get your hands on the money quickly. Choose between a **building society ordinary share account**, a **building society gold account**, a **bank deposit account**, a **bank cash card deposit account**, and a **bank high-interest cheque account**.

A building society is probably the best place to keep your emergency fund. Start saving with the simplest building society account – an **ordinary share account**. You can open an account with just £1 and you can put in and take out money as and when you want. There may be some restrictions on the amount you can take out in cash at branches other than the one where you keep your account.

When you have enough money, transfer it to a building society high interest account – often called a **gold account**. These pay a higher rate of interest on larger deposits. Many start at around £500. Some have a tiered interest rate: the more you invest the higher the interest rate. But check there are no penalties for taking your money out at short notice. Shop around for the best rate of interest. If you have a regionally-based building society near you, you may find they offer a higher rate of interest than the big national societies.

The other alternative is to open a **bank deposit account**. Again you can open one of these accounts with just £1, and you can deposit money whenever you like. But you lose seven days' interest if you take money out on demand, which is why the account is often known as a 7-day account.

A better bet could be one of the **cash card deposit accounts** offered by National Westminster, Lloyds and Royal Bank of Scotland. You get a cash card which you use to get cash over the counter or through a cash dispenser. The schemes vary in their detail. Find the one which suits your circumstances. The interest rate is usually the same as the bank deposit rate.

Or you could open a **bank high-interest cheque account**. The account pays interest like a deposit account, but you usually need to deposit at least £1,000 to open the account. Unlike a deposit account you get a cheque book.

Knowing the best place to save often flows from your reasons for saving. Be clear as to why you are saving, how long for, and which of your projects take priority. Once you have answers you can reduce the choice to a handful of schemes.

SHORT-TERM SAVINGS

Start with **short-term** savings, let's say anything less than a year. Maybe this year you don't want to run out of cash while you are on holiday, or end up in debt after the big Christmas spend. Avoid putting your money into a savings scheme which only starts giving of its best after the first year. You will be all right if you stick to any of the accounts you use for your emergency fund.

Or you could try a **National Savings Investment Account.** You can open one of these accounts at the Post Office with just £5. There is no commitment to save a regular amount, you can put in money as and when you like. Getting money out isn't so easy: you must give National Savings a month's notice whenever you want to make a withdrawal. This makes it an unsuitable vehicle for your emergency fund. But with holiday savings or large purchases, you know in advance when you will need the money, so this isn't too much of a disadvantage.

The interest rate on National Savings Investment Accounts is usually competitive with building society ordinary share accounts. But there is one difference: building societies and banks deduct basic-rate tax from all interest payments. This is not the case with National Savings and the interest on Investment Accounts is paid gross without any deduction for tax. This is useful for people who don't pay tax. If you are a taxpayer you must declare the interest payments to the Inland Revenue.

Don't confuse the National Savings Investment Account with the **Ordinary Account.** This is the old-fashioned Post Office account, that old favourite of aunts and godmothers hell bent on encouraging habits of thrift among the young. I still have the one my godmother opened for me when I was five. It contains the princely sum of £1. You can withdraw up to £100 on demand from a National Savings Ordinary Account. But the interest rate is low. Ironically, the people who benefit most are not all those nephews, nieces and godchildren, but rich grown-ups who pay income tax at higher than the basic rate of tax. In each tax year the first £70 worth of interest is tax-free, which can give an attractive rate of return to higher-rate taxpayers. Anyone else should leave these accounts alone.

MEDIUM-TERM SAVINGS

Saving for the **medium term** is anything longer than a year, but not more than five years. Almost anything could fall into this category – a holiday in some longed-for paradise the other side of the globe, a summer break from work, a deposit on your first house, or a financial cushion to soften the blow of going freelance.

Your choice is now very wide. If you are saving for a deposit on a house, make sure you keep some of your savings with at least a couple of building societies. With the banks tripping over themselves in the rush to hand out mortgages, you might wonder why you still have to bother saving with building societies at all. The banks blow hot and cold over mortgages and it might happen that you want a mortgage when the banks have cooled on the idea. And while it's true the building societies are looking more and more like banks these days, mortgage lending still remains their core business.

When you are saving for a deposit on a house, choosing a building society is not just a question of finding the highest interest rate. You also want to know if they will give you a mortgage when you need it. If you think you will only ever be able to afford to buy somewhere if you club together with a friend or group of friends, make sure the building societies you save with are prepared to lend on this basis. If it's your dream to start your own business, and find somewhere you can live and work, check they will lend on a mixed residential/commercial property. If you are itching to spend five years in overalls picking out a century of paint from decorative ceiling roses, then you must find out how keen they are to lend to gentrifiers.

Where else can you squirrel your money away if you are saving for between one and five years? All the accounts I have already mentioned are fine. But you can also investigate **National Savings Deposit Bonds, Yearly Plans, Index-Linked Certificates, Savings Certificates; building society subscription share accounts, Save-As-You-Earn accounts, notice accounts, term shares; bank monthly savings accounts, high-interest deposit accounts, notice accounts and term accounts.**

To get the best out of **National Savings Deposit Bonds**, you must hold them for at least a year. The minimum investment is £100, and you must give three months' notice when you want your money back. If you ask for your money back in the first year the interest rate is halved. The rate of interest is usually better than the bank deposit rate, but not as good as building society gold accounts. The interest is paid gross with no deduction for tax, but the interest is taxable and you must tell the Inland Revenue. Best for non-taxpayers.

If you want to commit yourself to saving a regular amount of money each month, you could try a **National Savings Yearly Plan**. With this scheme you save a regular amount each month for a year, and you can then leave the money to grow for another four years. You can save between £20 and £200 a month in multiples of £5. You get no interest until you have saved for 12 months. The rate of interest increases the longer you hold the plan. The highest rate of return, 7 per cent, is achieved if you hold the plan for five years. The rate is fixed when you start the plan. It takes around two weeks to get your money back. The interest is tax-free and you don't need to declare it on your tax return. For basic-rate taxpayers, the rate of interest usually compares favourably with other regular savings plans from the building societies or banks. But best of all for higher-rate taxpayers.

With **National Savings Index-Linked Certificates** your savings are linked to the Retail Price Index. Introduced in the 1970s when inflation was running well into double figures, they were originally restricted to savers over retirement age, which is how they got nicknamed 'Granny Bonds'. When inflation came down, they fell from favour, and when the 2nd issue was introduced the certificates were made available to everyone. And to keep them competitive, a bonus was added on top of the rate of inflation.

The 4th issue is the one currently available. They are available in units of £25 and you can hold just one unit. The maximum holding in the 4th issue is £5,000. You must hold them for a year to get the benefit of the index-linking. A yearly bonus is paid on top of the rate of inflation. The bonus increases the longer you hold the certificates. The first year's bonus is 3 per cent, the second year's is 3.25 per cent, the third year's 3.5 per cent, the fourth year's 4.5 per cent, the fifth year's 6 per cent. They are tax-free and you don't need to declare them to the taxman. Best for the higher-rate taxpayer.

National Savings Certificates are similar to Granny Bonds, only you get a rate of interest which is fixed with each issue rather than inflation-linked. Each certificate costs £25 and the amount you can hold varies between £1,000 and £10,000, depending on the issue. To get the full benefit you must hold the certificates for at least five years, as the interest rate is on a sliding scale. You start earning interest after the first year, but at a fairly modest level. The interest rate increases at the end of each year, reaching its maximum after five years. The interest is paid when you cash in the certificates. The current issue, the 33rd, gives an annual return of 7 per cent if you hold it for five years. The maximum investment is only £1,000, or £5,000 if you are investing the proceeds of a previous issue. The interest is tax-free and the taxman doesn't need to know about it. Best for higher-rate taxpayers.

The building societies have two regular savings schemes:

With **building society subscription shares** – they are also marketed under such names as Bonus Shares and Money-Builder – you undertake to pay a certain sum into your account each month and in return you get a slightly higher rate of interest than with an ordinary share account. Building societies vary, but the minimum monthly saving is usually between £1 and £10 a month. Most societies allow you to make between one and three partial withdrawals each year. If you make more, the account is either closed or the interest rate is reduced, depending on the society. Basic-rate tax is already deducted, but interest must be declared. Best for basic-rate taxpayers.

The other building society regular savings scheme – the **Save-As-You-Earn (SAYE) 2nd issue** – is really only suitable for higher-rate taxpayers who are prepared to save for at least five years. With this scheme you agree to pay between £1 and £20 a month. At the end of five years you get a tax-free bonus worth 14 of your monthly payments. If you keep your money invested for a further two years, the bonus is doubled. Worked out as an annual rate of return the bonus is worth 8.3 per cent after five years and 8.6 per cent after seven years.

If you are saving for a house, remember to register your savings scheme under the Government's **Homeloan Scheme**. You can register bank savings schemes as well as those with building societies. If you are registered under the Homeloan Scheme for at least two years before you buy your first home, you may qualify for a grant of £110 and an extra £600 of mortgage loan, interest-free for the first five years. To qualify for the grant you need to have at least £1,000 in your savings account for the whole of the year before you apply for a mortgage. To qualify for the interest-free mortgage loan, you must have at least £600 in your account when you apply. Ask your bank or building society for details or write to the Department of the Environment, Room N21/21, 2 Marsham Street, London SW1 3EB.

Building society notice and term accounts have been eclipsed by the development of gold accounts – high-interest accounts with instant access. However, if you are out to find the very highest rate of building society return you are still most likely to get it from a **notice** or **term account**.

These accounts are not suitable for the small regular saver as the minimum investment is high. With notice accounts it is often as high as £500; with term accounts it is between £1,000 and £2,000. The rate of interest goes up and down with building society rates and is usually between $1\frac{1}{2}$ and $2\frac{1}{2}$ per cent above the ordinary share rate. It is this differential which is often guaranteed. The actual interest rate rarely is. Notice accounts can be for anything between seven days and six months. This is the amount of notice you must give the building society when you want your money back. You can have it back sooner but you will lose interest, equivalent to the full notice period.

With term accounts you agree to leave your money deposited for a predetermined length of time. Depending on what's on offer, it could be as short as six months, or as long as five years. The rate of interest is occasionally guaranteed with term accounts of a year or less. You get your money back at the end of the term. If you want it back sooner, you must normally give three months' notice, and you usually lose three months' interest.

With both schemes basic-rate tax is deducted at source. Best for basic-rate taxpayers.

Not all banks operate **regular savings schemes**. Barclays, National Westminster, Royal Bank of Scotland, TSB and the Co-op offer them. With all these accounts you agree to save a certain amount each month. The rate of interest is slightly higher than on a bank 7-day deposit account. The minimum investment is usually £10 a month. National Westminster have a mortgage savings account which guarantees you a mortgage when mortgage funds are in short supply.

With regular monthly savings accounts, you must save for at least a year to qualify for the higher rate of interest. Withdrawals are discouraged, and you may lose interest if you insist on taking money out. The interest is paid with an amount for basic-rate tax already deducted. Best for basic-rate taxpayers.

Bank high-interest deposit accounts. These accounts are the banks' equivalent of building society gold accounts. In return for a high minimum deposit, your money earns extra interest. The minimum investment is between £1,000 and £10,000. Like bank deposit accounts, you must give seven days' notice when you want your money back. If you want immediate access you lose seven days' interest. Basic-rate tax is deducted from the interest payments. Best for basic-rate taxpayers.

Bank notice and **term accounts** work in much the same way as those offered by the building societies, although the minimum investment is usually higher – between £1,000 and £5,000 for notice accounts, between £500 and £5,000 for term accounts. The notice periods vary between three weeks and six months. The rate of interest on notice accounts is variable and is fixed in relation to the 7-day deposit rate. With bank term accounts you can lock up your money for between one month and two years. Unlike building society term accounts the rate of interest is guaranteed for the full term. Both accounts have tax at the basic rate deducted at source. Most suitable for basic-rate taxpayers.

LONG-TERM SAVINGS

Many of these accounts will serve you well if you want to save for the **long term** – periods of longer than five years. The idea is to start small and when you have enough money transfer it into a higher interest account, while always keeping your eye open for the interest rate bargain.

Or you can be more ambitious and think about putting a

first tentative toe into the world of stocks and shares. The best way of starting life as a stock market investor is through a **unit trust.**

Unit trusts take money from investors and pool it into a large fund. The people managing the fund then buy a selection of shares which they think will perform well. When you invest in a unit trust you buy units in the fund. The price of these units goes up and down depending on the fortunes of the shares in the fund.

Unit trusts are only suitable if you are saving for the long term. Because the value of your investment can go down as well as up, you want to avoid cashing units while the stock market is in decline. However, if you can keep your investment going for at least seven years, the evidence suggests that you may do better with a unit trust than with National Savings, building societies or a bank.

Most unit trusts ask for a minimum investment of between £200 and £1,000. But you can invest with less if you are prepared to save a regular amount each month. Most groups now offer regular savings schemes where the minimum investment can be as low as £10 a month. Look for a unit trust group which doesn't impose extra charges on their regular savers.

If you started putting £20 a month into a building society five years ago, you would have saved £1,200 and it would now be worth £1,458. But you would have done much better putting your money into a unit trust savings plan. The same monthly investment in an average-performing UK unit trust would be worth £2,387.

The difference becomes even more striking the longer you carry on saving. If you started saving £20 a month, 15 years ago, you would have saved £3,600 and your building society account would be worth £7,107. But if you had invested in an average UK trust it would be worth £18,446.

But it is important to realise that unit trust prices do go down as well as up. And these figures were produced at the beginning of April 1987 at a time when most of the world's stock markets were reaching new highs.

The income from unit trusts is paid after a deduction for basic-rate tax. Many unit trusts have accumulation units which add the income to the value of the units. Others allow you to use the income to buy extra units, for which there is usually a small charge.

When you put your money in a unit trust savings scheme you benefit from something called 'pound cost averaging'. It is something of a statistical freak. But because the price of units goes up and down, your money buys a different number of units each month. When the price goes down you buy more, when it rises you buy less. As a result, you end up buying more units than you would if the price of your units had stayed the same.

Choosing a unit trust is a daunting task – there are now at least 1,000 to choose from. There are unit trusts to feed everyone's investment fantasies. Trusts for seekers after a high income, trusts for those looking for capital appreciation, trusts investing in smaller companies, trusts investing in America, Japan, Europe – the list is almost endless. Unless you are prepared to do a lot of research, your first job is finding a unit trust group with a good investment record. You can ask your bank manager, but he is likely to channel you into one of the bank's own unit trusts. With one or two exceptions unit trusts run by the clearing banks have a mediocre investment record.

A trust's past performance is not necessarily a guide to how well it will do in the future, which is why your best bet is to choose your fund manager first. The two specialist magazines, *Planned Savings*, 33–35 Bowling Green Lane, London EC1R 0DA, tel: 01-837 1212, and *Money Management*, Greystoke Place, Fetter Lane, London EC4 1ND, tel: 01-405 6969, are a good place to start your search. You may find them in your local library. They publish performance figures which should point you in the direction of the fund managers with a good record. *The Independent* is another helpful source of information on unit trusts.

Unit trust savings schemes are extremely flexible. Most allow you to cash in units whenever you like, so long as your holding doesn't drop below a certain level – usually between £100 and £200. You can normally sell units over the telephone. Some managers pay up immediately, others wait until the end of the Stock Exchange account, which usually lasts two weeks.

Personal Equity Plans (PEP for short) are another possibility. These plans were introduced to encourage the growth of individual share ownership, and offer certain tax concessions. Regular savers can invest between £25 and £200 a month in a PEP. Lump sum investors are restricted to a ceiling of £2,400 a year. Under a PEP, dividend income is tax-free, and there is no Capital Gains Tax to pay when you sell the shares under your plan. Always check the charges; you can find yourself paying almost as much to your PEP manager as you are saving in tax.

You can only get a PEP from an approved PEP manager. Many banks, unit trust groups and insurance companies offer them. Looked at over the short term the tax concessions don't seem generous. But for higher-rate taxpayers, and anyone investing for the long term, the tax-free dividend payments can amount to a significant saving.

Some unit trust regular savings plans qualify for the PEP tax concessions. You are limited to £35 a month. But if you have decided to take out a unit trust regular savings plan anyway, check if you can do it through a PEP plan.

WILL I BE TEMPTED?

If you have a taste for the beautiful, the frivolous, and the luxurious, your resolve is likely to slip at the merest sight of it. You know you will suffer what the psychologists call PPD – post-purchase depression – but you still can't resist the temptation.

You need help to keep on the straight and narrow. Begin by trying to remember the number of times in the last year you have bought largish items which you later regretted. If you can establish a pattern, you will know how the damage is done and where to go window shopping at your peril.

The next trick is to save your money where you can't get hold of it easily, or where there are heavy penalties if you do take it out. Regular savings plans are a good way of forcing you to save, and most schemes positively discourage you from taking out too much money. If you are chasing the highest interest rates, notice and term accounts are better for you than accounts which offer instant access. And don't forget the National Savings Investment Account where you must give a month's notice if you want to get money out.

WHAT'S MY TAX POSITION?

You ignore your tax position at your peril. The best place for a higher-rate taxpayer to save her money won't necessarily be the same for a basic-rate taxpayer. And if you don't pay tax at all, your decision will be different again.

Banks and building societies both now pay interest with tax at the basic rate already deducted. If you don't pay tax, you can't claim the tax back. This usually means that banks and building societies are unsuitable places to put your money if you don't pay tax. Basic-rate taxpayers have nothing extra to pay. Higher-rate taxpayers get an extra tax bill. Building society Save-As-You-Earn schemes are the only exception – these are tax-free.

No tax is deducted from any National Savings scheme and some plans are actually tax-free. Those which are tax-free appeal mainly to higher-rate taxpayers. The interest rate may look low, but as the return they get on other investments is reduced by big tax bills they don't generally mind.

Where National Savings interest is taxable, the rate for basic-rate taxpayers is usually competitive with the banks and building societies. But with no tax deducted they offer the best return to those who pay no tax. Higher-rate taxpayers should concentrate on National Savings Ordinary Accounts, 4th Index-Linked Certificates, 33rd issue Savings Certificates, and Yearly Plans. Non-taxpayers do particularly well from Deposit Bonds and Investment Accounts.

When you save with a unit trust regular savings plan you expect the greater part of your growth to come from the rising value of your units rather than from their income. Even so, there is tax to pay on the dividend or income. It is paid, or added to your account, after an amount for basic-rate tax has been deducted. Non-taxpayers can claim this tax back. Basic-rate taxpayers have nothing extra to pay. Higher-rate taxpayers get an extra tax bill. The unit trust manager sends you a tax voucher which shows the dividend and the amount of tax deducted, called a tax credit. Enter this information on your tax return. Higher-rate taxpayers can keep their tax bill down by choosing a unit trust which pays a low income.

Here for quick reference is a ready reckoner covering all the savings schemes already mentioned. It shows the minimum and maximum investment, whether it is suitable for regular savings or larger lump sums, or both. It tells you if you can get your hands on your money at short notice, or if you lose interest if you do, or whether access is restricted. You can also see which taxpayer they suit best: non-taxpayer, basic-rate taxpayer or higher-rate taxpayer, and whether the interest rate is fixed or variable.

SAVINGS SUMMARY

National Savings Ordinary Account: Min £1, Max £10,000. Short term, regular savings and lump sums, instant access up to £100, rate variable. Best for higher-rate taxpayers.

National Savings Investment Account: Min £5, Max £50,000. Short term, regular savings and lump sums, restricted access, rate variable. Best for non-taxpayers.

National Savings Index-Linked Savings Certificates: Min £25, Max £5,000. Medium and long term, regular and lump sums, restricted access, rate variable. Best for higher-rate taxpayers.

National Savings Certificates – 33rd issue: Min £25, Max £1,000. Medium and long term, regular savings and lump sums, restricted access, fixed interest. Best for higher-rate taxpayers.

National Savings Yearly Plan: Min £20 a month, Max £200. Medium term, regular savings, restricted access, fixed interest. Best for higher-rate taxpayers.

National Savings Deposit Bonds: Min £100, Max £50,000. Medium term, lump sums, restricted access, fixed interest. Best for non-taxpayers.

Building society ordinary share account: Min £1, Max none. Short term, regular savings and lump sums, instant access, rate variable. Best for basic-rate taxpayers.

Building society subscription shares: Min £1 to £10 a month, Max £100 to £250 a month. Medium term, regular savings, restricted access, variable interest. Best for basic-rate taxpayers.

Building society Save-As-You-Earn (SAYE): Min £1 a month, Max £20 a month. Medium and long term, regular savings, restricted access, fixed interest. Best for higher-rate taxpayers.

Building society gold account: Min £250 to £1,000. Short and medium term, lump sums, instant access, variable interest. Best for basic-rate taxpayers.

Building society notice account: Min £100, Max none. Medium term, lump sums, immediate access but with loss of interest, variable interest. Best for basic-rate taxpayers.

Building society term account: Min £1,000 to £2,000, Max none. Medium term, lump sums, restricted access, variable interest, occasionally fixed. Best for basic-rate taxpayers.

Bank 7-day deposit account: Min £1, Max none. Short and medium term, regular savings and lump sums, immediate access but with loss of interest, variable interest. Best for basic-rate taxpayers.

Bank regular monthly savings account: Min £10 a month, Max none. Medium term, regular savings, restricted access, variable interest. Best for basic-rate taxpayers.

Bank high-interest deposit account: Min £1,000 to £10,000, Max none. Short and medium term, lump sums, immediate access but with loss of interest, variable interest. Best for basic-rate taxpayers.

Bank high-interest cheque account: Min £1,000 to £2,500, Max none. Short and medium term, lump sum, immediate access, variable interest. Best for basic-rate taxpayers.

Bank notice account: Min £1,000 to £5,000, Max none. Short and medium term, lump sums, immediate access but with loss of interest, variable interest. Best for basic-rate taxpayers.

Bank term account: Min £500 to £5,000, Max none. Short and medium term, lump sums, restricted access, fixed interest. Best for basic-rate taxpayers.

Unit trust regular savings plan: Min £10 to £50 a month, Max none. Long term, regular savings, restricted access, variable interest. OK for all taxpayers.

Finding the best rate of interest can be hard work. Start with the Saturday newspapers. The *Daily Telegraph*, *Guardian*, *Independent* and *Times* all list the different types of investment and the rates of interest, and all except the *Guardian* show the return at different rates of tax. However, none of these lists are much help if you want to know which building societies are paying the highest rates of interest. Here you are on your own. Gather up as much information from the building societies in your high street as you can, and keep an eye open for advertisements in the financial pages of the national newspapers.

For unit trust information, *Planned Savings*, *Money Management* and *The Independent* are your best sources. On Saturday *The Independent* publishes a list of unit trusts divided into their specialities: UK General, North American, Far East & Australia, International Growth, etc, and ranks them by one-year performance. It also shows the size of each trust and the minimum lump sum investment. *The Sunday Times* publishes an index of unit trust performance which gives you some idea of which specialities have done best in the past.

HOW SAFE IS MY INVESTMENT?

When you put your money in National Savings, you are effectively lending to the Government, and your savings are effectively guaranteed by the Government.

If you put your money on deposit with any UK bank or building society registered with the Building Society Registry you are covered by a statutory compensation scheme. If your bank or building society goes bust, you stand to get 90 per cent of your deposits up to £20,000. The moral is, don't invest more than £20,000 in any bank or building society unless you are convinced it's rock solid.

There is no compensation scheme for unit trust investors. But all unit trusts authorised by the Department of Trade and Industry are required to appoint an independent trustee who holds the unit trust investments. If a unit trust management company went bust, the trustee would return the value of the fund to the individual investors. It has never happened.

£££

3
Finding a bank manager

If the first rule of life is know thyself; the first rule of ordering your finances is know your bank manager. All the big banks are much of a muchness – you have to run a fine tooth comb through the small print to spot the differences. The service you get from your bank depends much more on the personality of your bank manager than the name over the bank door. So don't be lured into opening a bank account by cheap plastic wallets, pictures on your cheques, or cheap plastic biros. Look instead for a bank manager who can become your best financial friend.

Don't be one of those people who can't put a name, let alone a face to their bank manager. Most people only get to know their bank manager when something goes wrong, and the relationship is for ever soured by those early hostilities. If you are satisfied with the service you get from your bank, make a friend of your bank manager while everything is running smoothly.

But remember if your bank manager is making your life difficult, you can always sack him and change your bank or your bank branch. The banks rely on the fact that few people ever do, which is why the banks put so much effort into getting you through their doors at an early age.

If you do decide to start afresh, don't just take your account to the bank next door. Instead try and find a bank manager more to your taste. Ask around. Can any of your friends recommend their bank manager?

Seek out people who have gone cap in hand to their bank manager for money. What is his attitude to unusual mortgage deals? Is he good at helping small businesses get on their feet? And on a more mundane level, is he relaxed about handing out overdrafts?

Once you have bagged your man, check out his branch. Bank managers in small provincial towns have less status within their bank than those operating in the business quarter of a large city. The provincial bank manager may not be able to lend more than a quite modest amount without referring the decision to his regional office. The big city manager is likely to have much more freedom and autonomy.

Convenience is another factor. When you are just starting out it's hard to establish a good rapport with a bank manager if he is based somewhere on the other side of the country. On the other hand he doesn't need to be at your nearest branch either. After all, you don't have to call on your bank manager each time you want some cash – you can cash cheques up to £50 with a guarantee card at any branch of your bank for no charge. And if there is one branch you use a lot, you can have an arrangement to cash larger cheques there. And these days cash cards give you access to a network of cash dispensers.

Getting to know your bank manager is never a waste of time. As soon as you have opened an account, see if you can meet him. It doesn't matter what pretext you use. The bank may ask you to wait six months before giving you a cheque guarantee card. Go and argue the toss with your bank manager. You may not win the point, but at least you have made contact.

If you want your bank manager eating out of your hand, don't expect him to be a mind reader. Let him know what you are doing and why. Always make sure it's you and not your bank manager who makes the first move. If you think you need an overdraft for a couple of months, make the effort: go and see him and ask him for one. Apart from anything else, an authorised overdraft is cheaper than one which you run up without the bank's permission. And you are saved the bother of a terse letter.

Bank managers like to know their customers. Let yours think he has a special insight into your psychological make-up and he is much more likely to back your more ambitious projects.

And in those day-to-day areas where bank managers can use their discretion, you are much more likely to get yours to waive something like disputed bank charges if he feels you are basically on his side.

But the one thing above all others that bank managers can't abide is a disputatious customer. So if you do have a justified complaint about bank charges, say, be firm but keep the argument good humoured. Never indulge in that tempting sport – bank manager baiting. And never, unless you are thinking of changing your bank, write a letter of complaint to your bank manager's superior in the bank. Like your doctor, your relationship with your bank manager is personal and private.

The trouble with good bank managers is they are always on the move. You may have nurtured yours for five years only to find he is promoted to a better job. You are very happy for him, of course; it's just that this better job is 200 miles away. If you don't mind losing the face-to-face contact, there is nothing to stop you moving your account to your manager's new branch.

Developing a good relationship with your bank manager is the best way of overcoming the undoubted, and I suspect in many cases totally unconscious, bias banks have against women customers. Banks are very good at taking our money. But when it comes to lending us money they are not nearly so hot. Women hold 49 per cent of all bank current accounts, and 50 per cent of all deposit accounts. But when it comes to borrowing money we only have around 38 per cent of all bank lending[1].

No bank is tackling the problems which women have with their bank accounts. I'm convinced that women use their bank accounts differently from men. We won't carry around large amounts of cash for fear of being at best pickpocketed, at worse mugged. We probably write more cheques and for smaller amounts than men, who feel safer stuffing their wallets with notes. Not only does this cost us a lot of money each time we overdraw, it also costs the banks more to service our accounts. Which is probably why, with the exception of the Trustee Savings Bank – 'the bank that likes to say yes' – no bank has put much effort into wooing women, or cared to think about what we might want from a bank.

Instead of banks which understand our real needs, we get fobbed off with cheques printed over with pretty woodland scenes. As if that could make up for banks which aren't open when we need them, often charge us £1 to cash another bank's cheque, and still don't take us seriously when we want to borrow money, or start our own businesses.

Over the last 20 years, it is the building societies and not the banks which have exercised the greatest influence on our habits of saving. It took the banks a while to wake up to the fact. But in the early 1980s they responded by moving, in some cases very aggressively, into the mortgage market, where the building societies had hitherto reigned supreme. While this was happening more and more people were using their building society accounts like bank accounts as the queues in any building society branch on a Saturday morning testified.

A few building societies experimented with cheque accounts, and basically failed for want of being able to issue cheque guarantee cards. They were also slow to introduce cash dispensers, although being late to the game gave them the chance to put in more up-to-date machines. By the early months of 1987 the banks had nearly 7,000 cash dispensers whereas the building societies operated less than 1,500.

By the beginning of 1987 the rivalry between the banks and the building societies began to resemble a pitched battle with the Government handing the building societies the weapon which finally let them compete on equal terms for personal customers. It was called the Building Societies Act 1986 and for the first time the building societies could lend money which wasn't secured on property.

Now that the building societies have got so much going for them, why bother with a bank at all? Why not cultivate your building society manager instead? For the same reason you save with a building society if you want to buy a house, you go to the people who are best at banking. And regardless of all the changes, when it comes to transferring money from one person to another and lending it for things other than houses, the banks still do it best. But most important of all, you need a bank manager just in case you ever want to go it alone, or have a good business idea, because if your bank manager believes in you, his bank will back you up with money.

You will only get the best out of your bank and building society accounts once you start mastering the detail. Here's what you can expect, plus some tips to help you keep the upper hand in your dealings with these mighty financial institutions.

THE BANKS. WHO ARE THEY?

The four big-name high street banks are Barclays, Lloyds, Midland and National Westminster. Of the four, National Westminster has most branches – 3,200 – followed by Barclays and Lloyds with 2,900 and 2,300 respectively. Midland is the smallest with 2,200 branches.

Other banks which offer a similar banking service are the Co-operative, the Trustee Savings Bank, and the Scottish banks: the Bank of Scotland, Royal Bank of Scotland, Williams and Glyn's and the Clydesdale.

The National Girobank offers a slightly different service. The cheque cashing service is through the Post Office and you are not supposed to let your account go into the red.

WHAT DO THE BANKS CHARGE?

If you have a cheque account, you get free banking if you keep your account in credit. The banks rely on the fact that a lot of people find this difficult, because as soon as you overdraw by as much as a penny you are charged for everything in sight during a three-month period. As well as clocking up interest charges you are charged each time you write a cheque, pay a standing order or credit transfer. And to add insult to injury the bank will, like as not, charge you for sending you a threatening letter!

Lloyds and National Girobank come out best. Lloyds operates a monthly charging period rather than a three-monthly one. With Lloyds, if you overdraw, they only levy charges for that month, then wipe the slate clean again. With Girobank you only pay fees while you are overdrawn – which technically you are not allowed to be.

HOW TO AVOID BANK CHARGES?

Keep a very close watch on your balance. If you find it difficult to do the sums on your cheque stubs, ask your bank manager for monthly rather than three-monthly statements. If you are near your bank branch, you can call in and ask for a balance. But don't confuse the ledger balance with the cleared balance. Unless you ask for the cleared balance, you will be given the ledger balance and this could lull you into a false sense of security. Any money you pay in to your bank account appears on your ledger immediately. However, it won't show up on your cleared balance for at least three working days until the cheque is cleared through the banking system. So you could be overdrawn on your cleared balance, while your ledger balance was in credit. Bank charges are levied on the cleared balance, although you only pay interest charges on the ledger balance. You may also be able to order a bank statement through your nearest cash dispenser.

CHEQUE GUARANTEE CARDS

A cheque or current account is all but useless without a cheque guarantee card. Unless they know you, few shops will take a cheque unless you can guarantee it. The card guarantees cheques up to £50, so if you are spending more than £50 many shops now prefer you to pay by cash or credit card.

When you open a bank account you may have to wait six months before the bank gives you a cheque guarantee card – they want to see if you use your account responsibly. If they say six months, try asking for one after three months. At Barclays the system is different. The Barclaycard credit card also acts as a Barclays Bank cheque guarantee card and you can apply for a Barclaycard whenever you like whether or not you have an account with Barclays Bank. If you already have a Barclaycard you have a ready-made cheque guarantee card if you then open a cheque account with Barclays.

HELP, I'M OVERDRAWN!

If you go into the red by mistake there are several ways of keeping down the subsequent bank charges. Write as few cheques as possible. Use your credit card for most of your non-cash transactions and settle the bill at the end of the month with one cheque. If some of your bills arrive in a bunch, write one cheque for the total, make it out to the bank and let them sort it out.

HELP, I'M ALWAYS OVERDRAWN!

Before your bank manager loses his patience, attack him for an overdraft. An overdraft which you arrange with your bank manager is much cheaper than one which you take without asking. With an authorised overdraft, the rate of interest is likely to be between 3 and 5 per cent over bank base rate, an unauthorised overdraft is between 6 and 12 per cent over base rate.

But ask if there is an arrangement fee for setting up an overdraft. If there is and you don't intend being overdrawn for long, or by very much, you may be better off risking your bank manager's wrath with an unauthorised one. Avoid the half-way houses which some banks, notably Lloyds and National Westminster, are offering. As an alternative to an arranged overdraft your bank manager may offer you an agreed credit limit up to which you can overdraw whenever you like. The interest rate is pitched half-way between an authorised and an unauthorised overdraft. The main disadvantage is the encouragement it gives you to spend, spend, spend.

HELP, I SHOULDN'T BE OVERDRAWN

If you are one of those unfortunate people who is almost always in the black, but somehow never manages to keep up the good work for a whole three months, think about taking out a bank/building society linked account.

There are two accounts specially designed to prevent people like you being clobbered with bank charges – Alliance and Leicester BankSave linked with the Bank of Scotland, and Birmingham Midshires Mastercheque linked with the Trustee Savings Bank. Both schemes work in the same way. You pay your money, probably your monthly pay cheque, into a building society account. Each time your bank current account drops below a certain figure it is automatically topped up with a transfer from your building society account. You get a cheque book to use with your bank current account and the amount you are required to keep in the account is relatively modest. The interest on the deposit account is higher than on an ordinary building society share account.

HELP I'M IN SERIOUS DEBT

It's frighteningly easy to borrow money. A walk down any high street could produce at least half a dozen store credit cards; the newspapers are bursting with loan offers, and I, for one, am forever being induced to borrow money through the post.

Is it any wonder that people end up borrowing more money than they can afford to repay? If this happens to you, stay calm. The first step towards sorting yourself out is admitting you have a problem. The next is having the courage to write to your lenders and ask for help. Prepare a schedule of how much money you owe and your monthly repayments. Then work out how much you can afford to repay each month, and tell your lender this is the amount you are prepared to pay. By keeping them in the picture, they are much more likely to be sympathetic to the idea of accepting reduced payments than if you just default on the loan.

If this approach doesn't produce results, enlist the help of a debt counsellor. Your local branch of the Citizens Advice Bureaux can put you in touch with one of their specialists, or you could find your nearest Money Advice Centre by writing to the Money Advice Association, 318 Summer Lane, Birmingham B19 3RL.

If you have borrowed unwisely and expensively, investigate with your bank manager whether it's possible to reduce the cost of your borrowings by taking out a cheaper loan from your bank and using it to repay your outstanding loans. This only makes sense if the rate of interest is significantly lower and the terms for getting out of your existing loans are reasonable.

Avoid at all cost loans advertised specifically for this purpose. They are either expensive or they require you to offer your house as security.

OTHER WAYS OF BORROWING MONEY FROM THE BANK

Apart from mortgages, there are two further ways of borrowing money from a bank. There are **personal loans**, and **bank ordinary loans.** You can apply for a bank personal loan from any bank, it doesn't need to be the one you bank with. The loan is unsecured so the rate of interest is quite high – higher than an overdraft but lower than bank credit cards such as Access and Visa. These loans are used for larger purchases, things like cars, furniture and home improvements. The interest rate is arranged at the outset. The loan is for a fixed period, usually two, three or five years, and you repay the loan in equal monthly instalments.

But if you own your house and you aren't mortgaged up to the hilt, you can borrow more cheaply from the Midland if you are already a customer or don't mind moving your account there.

Bank ordinary loans also work out cheaper than personal loans because the bank asks for security. You can only get one of these loans from your own bank. The interest rate fluctuates in line with market rates. Bank ordinary loans are extremely flexible, and it's up to you to negotiate the terms with your bank manager. You can pay back the loan in equal monthly instalments, or in a lump sum at the end of an agreed period.

IS THERE TAX RELIEF ON BANK LOANS?

There is never any tax relief on overdrafts. But with any other loan, if you use the money to buy or improve your own home, you can claim tax relief, so long as your existing mortgage relief is not more than £30,000.

CAN I USE MY BUILDING SOCIETY LIKE A BANK?

This depends on your building society. In some ways building societies steal a march on the banks, in others they have chosen to lag behind. The best thing that can be said for building societies as banks is they stay open longer, and they are all open on the busiest shopping day of the week: Saturday. But in spite of now being able to operate their own cheque accounts with cheque guarantee cards, most building societies have been reluctant to go down that route, for fear of being buried under mounds of paper and a cost structure to match the banks. The exceptions are the Abbey National, the Nationwide and Town and Country. On the whole, the building societies have preferred to turn their attention to areas like estate agency and financial advice.

Personal loans are a different matter. Here the building societies are attacking the banks head on. Most of the big building societies are now offering personal loans on similar terms to the banks, although they are prevented from lending more than £5,000 unsecured. But if you own your house, you may be able to borrow more cheaply from your building society. Get them to quote you a rate of interest for a secured personal loan. This type of loan is usually only available when mortgage funds are plentiful.

DO I NEED MORE PLASTIC?

Cash cards are a useful way of increasing access to your bank or building society accounts. The number of cash dispensers is growing fast, as is the number of machines which will take other bank or building society cards. So even if you are unlikely to use the card today, it probably won't be long before you are close to a machine which will take at least one of the cards in your handbag. You can now use your Midland cash card in a National Westminster cash dispenser and vice versa. Lloyds, Barclays, Bank of Scotland and Royal Bank of Scotland cash dispensers all work with each other's cards.

There are two cash point machine networks run principally by the building societies. **Link** is a joint venture with around 1,000 machines led by the National Girobank, Co-operative Bank, Abbey National and Nationwide building societies. **Matrix** with 700 machines is led by seven major building societies, including the Alliance and Leicester, Anglia, Leeds and Woolwich, etc. The Halifax has developed its own system and has installed machines in the majority of its 850 branches.

With all these cash point machines you are sent a PIN – short for Personal Identification Number – just before you get your card. This is the secret code which allows you to get money out of a cash point machine. Try and remember this number. If you use your card infrequently you probably won't be able to, so be careful about where you keep a note of the number, preferably in code (try writing it backwards for example). Don't hand a thief the key to your bank account.

You can get a cash point card for a variety of accounts. The banks mainly offer them with cheque accounts, although some banks link them with 7-day deposit accounts as well. And if you have a PIN for your VISA or Access card, you can use these in the appropriate bank cash dispenser. Building societies either have special cash dispenser accounts, or more commonly attach them to existing share accounts. Some like the Abbey National have a cash dispenser card which can be used with their instant access high-interest account – the Five Star Account.

Apart from giving you money, all cash dispensers will tell you how much you have in your account. Others, especially those from the building societies, let you pay in money. You can even have a conversation with the more sophisticated machines. You can order a cheque book, tell them to send you a statement, and in the case of the Halifax, Nationwide and Woolwich building societies, pay your bills. Who knows, you may soon be able to send your bank manager a Valentine?

HOW SAFE ARE MY ACCOUNTS?

This is one area where the banks take a kindlier view of their customers than the building societies. By and large the banks don't make you suffer for any money which fraudulently disappears from your account when your cheque book, guarantee card or cash card are lost or stolen. But they do ask you to telephone your branch as soon as you realise something is missing, and then to confirm the loss in writing within three days.

They are not quite so generous with their credit cards. Here you may find yourself meeting the first £50 of any loss.

As a recently reported case with the Britannia building society demonstrated, building societies make their customers responsible for any loss if a passbook should fall into the wrong hands. In this case the passbook was an old one where the signature could be read by anyone. Make sure your building society passbooks are secure. Most building societies render your signature invisible except by the cashier with an ultra-violet light.

HOW DO I COMPLAIN?

If you have made the effort to get on with your bank manager, you shouldn't need to complain. But if it does reach fisty cuffs, stop at outright violence and take your case to the Banking Ombudsman. He only takes on cases if the bank's own complaints procedure is exhausted. The banks agree to be bound by his decision. But if you don't like his ruling you can pursue your case through the courts. He has power to make settlements of up to £50,000. You find the Banking Ombudsman at Citadel House, 5/11 Fetter Lane, London EC4A 1BR, tel: 01-583 1395.

The building societies operate a similar scheme. The building societies' ombudsman can be reached through the Building Societies Assocation, 3 Savile Row, London W1X 1AF, tel: 01-437 9655.

THE BANK OF THE FUTURE

In early 1987, as the building societies tussled with how they were to cope with their new-found freedoms, the Nationwide Building Society asked Joe Public to help them design the perfect bank account.

I know what I want. Some of my demands are what is in store for us anyway in the bank of the future. The rest are about keeping the good old-fashioned virtues of the personal touch. I long for the day when we can throw away our cheque books. They are bulky, they get dog-eared, you always forget to order a new one in time, they have a tendency to go missing, and cheques take a long time to process. I'm a convert to plastic money. The sooner the banks, building societies and retailers bring in fully electronic banking – what the experts call EFTPOS, Electronic Funds Transfer at Point of Sale – the better.

The bank account of tomorrow will have one card which you can use to withdraw cash, either through a cash dispenser or in a bank. When you go shopping you will be able to say whether the card is to be used to debit your current account, savings account or credit account. Barclays introduced a debit card in the summer of 1987, and after some initial resistance from the retailers the card can now be used in most shops displaying the VISA sign.

Bank charges should be simplified, and only levied when you are actually overdrawn. Banks should help those customers who don't want to run up bank charges by accident. Every bank should offer a linked account facility where a savings account is used to top up a current account whenever it looks in danger of going into the red.

An alternative is the system already offered by the TSB. If you bank with the TSB you can now electronically check your bank balance, pay bills and transfer funds between accounts at almost any time of the day and night. All you need is a telephone and a special tonepad similar in size to a TV remote control. The tonepad costs £12 and the TSB charge £2.50 a quarter for the service. Lloyds are experimenting with electronic banking. By the end of 1987, 1,000 Lloyds customers will be linked to the bank's computer via the telephone.

The pioneers of electronic banking are the Nottingham Building Society and Royal Bank of Scotland Homelink. But the system is expensive unless you already rent a Prestel set or have a facility for linking up your computer over the telephone.

I'm relying on the banks and building societies to make sure that all their systems are so secure that no computer genius can break into my account and get their sticky fingers on my money. If this is the case, and it still is a big if, all this electronic wizardry should mean that bank managers can spend more time getting to know their customers.

[1] NOP April–November 1986 survey of Women and Finance.

£££

4
The taxman

Marriage comes as a terrible shock, and not just emotionally. As a single woman you were financially independent, and you were expected to be responsible for your own tax affairs. Once you are married, the taxman reduces you to the status of a moron who has difficulty writing her name, and who wouldn't know her MIRAS from her P.60.

The problem lies with our tax laws. The British tax system is based on the family. And your tax life as a family starts when you get married. After that you and your husband, and to a certain extent your children under 18, are taxed as one. From now on your contribution to the family budget is reduced to a column on your husband's tax return. If you ever needed confirmation that society still secretly thinks of women as their husbands' chattel, this is it.

It was less than 10 years ago that married women won the right to correspond with the Inland Revenue on their own tax affairs. Before then, the Inland Revenue used to send the reply to her husband.

And the tax system continues to rob women of their privacy. Whatever we do, we still have a hard job keeping the state of our finances from our husbands because the taxman tells them everything. Even if we ask to have our tax assessed separately and fill in our own tax returns, our tax bills get sent to our husbands. The position is a bit better if we opt to be taxed separately. The problem is, most couples end up paying more tax if they do. Separate taxation is only of any use if both husband and wife earn a lot of money.

When I fill in my tax return it's my husband who gets the tax bill. I feel honour bound to pay it, and in return he gets to know how much I earn. It's not that I want to keep my earnings a secret. It's just that I think I have the same right to privacy as my husband.

To be fair to the Inland Revenue it's not entirely their fault either. They have to operate tax laws which were constructed while Beethoven was alive and which are now hopelessly out of touch with the reality of most people's lives in the 1980s.

And it cuts both ways, because while it renders women powerless and robs them of their financial independence, it also imposes tremendous burdens on men. In law it is the husband who is finally responsible for paying his wife's tax bill. So if you mismanage your affairs, the Inland Revenue goes after your husband, not you, for any unpaid tax. The Inland Revenue leaflet covering tax and marriage is IR31.

But the injustices don't end here. Most couples pay less tax once they walk down the aisle. But thanks to the **Married Man's Personal Allowance** it's the husband who normally collects the benefit in his pay packet, rarely the wife. This is another relic of that bygone age when married men were expected to keep home for a dependent wife, and society chose to reward them for their sacrifice through the tax system. The Married Man's Personal Allowance is the higher tax allowance which men claim once they are married.

In the 1987–88 tax year, the Married Man's Personal Allowance was worth £3,795, compared with the Single Person's Allowance of £2,425. Just by getting married a man who pays basic-rate tax gets an extra £31 a month in his pay packet.

There are two ways of mitigating this unequal sharing out of the tax goodies. One is to consider **Separate Assessment**. The other is only worth while if you and your husband are both high earners. It's called the **Wife's Earned Income Election**. Under this system your earnings are taxed separately and you may save a lot of tax.

It's easy to confuse separate assessment with separate taxation.

Separate assessment makes no difference to your final tax bill, separate taxation can save you hundreds of pounds.

Separate assessment carves up a couple's joint tax allowances in accordance with their separate earnings. Both husband and wife get a tax return, and each is then legally liable for his or her share of tax. To qualify for separate assessment ask for leaflet IR32 and fill in Inland Revenue form 11S in the six months before 6 July. To have got separate assessment for the tax year 1987–88 you needed to apply between 6 January and 6 July 1987. You don't need to ask your husband before applying for separate assessment, and he can apply for it too without asking you. Once you ask for separate assessment you continue to be taxed on this basis until you ask for the method to be changed.

Getting married and earning a lot of money don't go together. This is where separate taxation, or the Wife's Earned Income Election, can save you from mounting tax bills. When you get married your income is added to that of your husband. This can quite easily lumber you (or strictly speaking your husband) with a bill for higher-rate tax, even though as two separate people you only paid tax at the basic rate.

With separate taxation your earnings, but not your investment income, are taxed as if you were still two single people, and you continue to collect the tax allowances to which you were entitled as single people. Under this method your husband gives up his right to claim the Married Man's Personal Allowance. This makes the calculation quite complicated. In some cases you pay less tax as a couple if you continue to claim the Married Man's Personal Allowance even though you end up paying a small amount of higher-rate tax. This is because in marginal cases the amount of money you lose by giving up the higher Married Man's Personal Allowance is less than the amount of higher-rate tax you save by being taxed separately.

Take as an example the 1987–88 tax year. As a rule of thumb you needed a joint income of at least £26,870, with the lower earner contributing at least £6,545, before it was worth opting for separate taxation. The higher your joint earnings, the less the lower earner needed to contribute. But it was not worth claiming if the lower earner brought in less than £4,915.

You can make the Wife's Earned Income Election up to 12 months after the end of the tax year. Unlike Separate Assessment, both partners need to sign the form. Ask the Inland Revenue for form 14, and leaflet IR13. You continue to be taxed separately until you ask for it to be withdrawn, which you can do on form 14-1, again up to 12 months after the end of the tax year.

When Maggie and Roy Griffin got married in July 1984, they didn't realise they had to share the happy event with their tax office. They are both comfortably off. Roy is an Assistant Secretary in the civil service; Maggie at that time worked as a BBC executive. It was two years before they discovered the tax significance of their marriage. Maggie remembers with horror the day she rang her tax office only to be told she and Roy might face an extra tax bill of around £400 because once their two incomes were added together they became liable to higher-rate tax. Luckily the taxman had made a mistake. Maggie and Roy made the Wife's Earned Income Election with around six months to spare.

This is because women are taxed as if they are single in the tax year in which they marry, and you have until the end of the following tax year in which to ask to be taxed separately. In Maggie and Roy's case, Maggie was taxed as a single woman in the 1984–85 tax year. The following tax year (1985–86) they should have been taxed together, but they made the Wife's Earned Election in plenty of time – in their case before 6 April 1987.

The taxman has a soft spot for couples in the year of their marriage. As already explained, women are taxed as single people in the tax year of their marriage, unless they decide to get married on 6 April. But your husband is treated as being married from the day he seals the knot. He can claim the higher Married Man's Personal Allowance as soon as he gets married, although he only gets the full allowance if you marry before May 5. If you marry later in the tax year the allowance is reduced on a sliding scale, but it can never be less than the Single Person's Personal Allowance.

Houseowners can expect a big bonus. If you both own your own houses before you get married, you get tax relief on the mortgage interest payments while you sell your houses, and this continues for up to a year after you get married. And if you decide to buy a house jointly you get tax relief on those mortgage payments as well. So for the year after you get married you can, in theory, own three houses, and claim mortgage interest relief on loans of up to £30,000 on each one, a possible total of £90,000.

Investment income is the other big bone of contention for women taxpayers. Your investments might be nice little earners before you get married, but once you pass over the marriage threshold it all changes. They are still your investments, but the taxman gives the income to your husband, and taxes it at his top-rate of tax.

And that's not all. If your only source of income is from your investments, you lose your right to a personal tax allowance once you get married. When you are single you can set the Single Person's Personal Allowance against your investment income. As soon as you get married, you claim the Wife's Earned Income Allowance instead. This is just what it says it is – an allowance against earned income. You can't set it against investment income.

And there is no wriggling out of this one. You cannot opt for separate taxation on your investment income. Whatever you do, you are taxed together. Whether you inherit wealth or accumulate it through your own thrift and investment cunning, marriage is bad news for the independently wealthy woman. If investment income is your only source of income, marriage robs you of your personal tax allowance, and you are better off unmarried.

And it's not just women with private incomes who think twice before getting married. Rocketing house prices, especially in London and the South East, has made marriage an expensive luxury for a lot of couples. At the end of 1986, the cost of an average house in greater London stood at nearly £65,000[1] and as a result mortgages of £60,000 plus are not uncommon.

A couple who stay single can each claim the maximum tax relief of £30,000. With tax at 27 per cent, and the mortgage rate at $11\frac{1}{4}$ per cent, the tax relief on a £30,000 mortgage is worth £911 a year, nearly £76 a month, more if you pay higher-rate tax. Once you get married you are treated as one unit for tax purposes and are restricted to mortgage tax relief of £30,000 and no more. If you have previously been claiming two sets of mortgage tax relief, you are effectively awarding yourself a pay cut of at least £911 a year by getting married, which is a powerful incentive to remain in blissful sinfulness.

There are further benefits if you then decide to have children. One-parent families are entitled to an additional tax allowance – **The Additional Personal Allowance.** This is the allowance which makes up the difference between the Single Person's Personal Allowance and the Married Man's Allowance. In the 1987–88 tax year it stood at £1,370. You don't have to be a single parent to claim this allowance. If you are an unmarried couple with a child, one of you can claim the allowance or you can agree to share it. If you have two or more children you can each claim the full allowance. But you can't claim more than one allowance each, even if you have more than two children.

Everyone is entitled to tax allowances, even a new-born child. If you are living with someone and have children, you can apply to the Magistrates Court for an **affiliation order** under which your partner agrees to pay a yearly amount to help support each child. Money given to a child under an affiliation order is tax-free so long as it doesn't exceed the level of the child's personal tax allowance. This is another of those instances where the direct effect is felt in your partner's pay packet rather than your own. But you can probably argue the case for a share out.

However, affiliation proceedings are likely to bite the dust once the Family Law Reform Bill is implemented. This is the bill which seeks to increase the legal status of illegitimate children. Once it becomes law, the right of married women to apply to the County Court for financial support for their children will be extended to unmarried women.

There is one curious quirk in the workings of the tax system which actually benefits women. If you are married and your husband doesn't work, or doesn't earn enough to use up all his Married Man's Personal Allowance, you can claim his allowance as well as your own. If the reverse is the case, and it's you who stays at home, your husband can't claim your unused personal allowance. So if you and your husband earn about the same, and one of you wants to stay at home and look after the children, the family is better off financially if you go to work and leave your husband at home with the washing up and nappies.

But many women face a struggle when they try and claim the Married Man's Personal Allowance. Dot Palmer-Fry works as an executive in an oil company, while her husband Mike looks after their three young boys. It took Dot three months to persuade her tax office that she was entitled to her husband's tax allowance. Even her accountant failed and she only succeeded after enlisting the help of the Equal Opportunities Commission.

TAX REFORM

The Government has proposed sweeping changes to the way men and women are taxed. In 1986 it published a Green Paper (The Reform of Personal Taxation, Cmnd 9756 HMSO) which put forward a new system of separate taxation. The idea is to shift the unit of personal taxation from the family to the individual.

Under these proposals the Married Man's Personal Allowance and the Wife's Earned Income Allowance cease to exist. Instead, everyone, regardless of sex and marital status, gets the same basic tax allowance. In addition, the investment income of married women is no longer treated as her husband's. This means that women who live on investment income don't lose their personal tax allowance when they get married, because they no longer require a source of earned income to qualify for a personal allowance.

So far so good, and up to this point the proposals are good news for women. With the move to separate taxation the tax system should no longer discriminate against women.

Unfortunately the proposals don't end there. As they stand, most married couples are worse off. And with the abolition of the Married Man's Personal Allowance, it's the nation's husbands who would bear the brunt of the change – in their pay packets.

The Government expected squeals of agony, so it suggested a system of transferable allowances. Under this proposal, a married person can transfer any unused personal allowance to his or her partner. So a married couple with only one partner working is entitled to claim the same allowances as a married couple where both partners are working.

Transferable allowances are fine in theory. In practice they discriminate against women. They remove some of the financial incentive to get back to work after a break to look after children or ageing parents – a position women find themselves in more frequently than men. When you do return to work, the family is no better off until you earn more than your personal allowance. Even then the family loses at least 27p in tax on every pound of its second income. Some women see it as a plot to keep them tied to the kitchen sink. Whatever the thinking behind the proposals, it is estimated that 200,000 fewer married women will choose to work.

Women with domineering husbands are likely to experience particular problems because the decision to go back to work hits them in their pay packets. Once back at work your personal tax allowance is transferred from your husband to you and he ends up with less in his pay packet. You can just imagine the rows!

There is another proposal to limit the tax relief on mortgage interest payments to £30,000 for each property rather than each person as at present. It may not be fair that wealthy unmarried couples are at such a financial advantage over their married equals. But it will also make it much more expensive for single women wanting to buy property to share, especially in high-cost areas like London and the South East.

These changes are for the future and the detail is still being argued out. The Government has even indicated that it doesn't put a very high priority on the introduction of individual taxation. So it looks as if we are going to have to live with the present system with all its injustices for a good number of years yet.

DOING YOUR OWN TAX

The tax system may be a many-headed monster, but it is best to understand the nature of the beast. It's actually not as complex as it seems. But if you haven't mastered its ins and outs you may be wasting money. If your tax affairs are simple you may be paying too much tax to the Inland Revenue without knowing it. If they are more complicated you may be paying an accountant hundreds of pounds each year, for something you can probably do better yourself.

Start by getting to know the five vital tax documents:

○ **P.45:** This is the document you need when you start a new job. It gives your new employer all the information he needs to start taxing you correctly. If you don't have it, your employer puts you on an emergency code, and you are likely to end up paying too much tax. You get a P.45 from your previous employer, or from your unemployment office if you are signing off.

○ **P.60:** Your employer will give you one of these soon after the end of the tax year, which runs from 6 April in one year to 5 April in the next year. It shows how much you earned during the tax year, your taxable income, and how much tax your employer deducted from your pay packet. Keep this document safe, because your employer is not required to give you a copy if you lose it.

○ **Notice of Coding:** If you work for an employer and pay tax through the Pay-As-You-Earn system (PAYE for short), the Inland Revenue sends you one of these in February or March each year. It sets out the tax allowances to which you are entitled. Check it. If it's correct you are unlikely to be paying too much tax.

○ **Tax Return:** You only get a tax return if your finances are relatively complicated, you are self-employed or you ask for one. You probably don't need an accountant to fill it in. And if you keep good financial records thoughout the year, it shouldn't take you long to complete.

○ **Notice of assessment:** This is effectively your tax bill. Again you only get one if your finances are fairly complicated. It tells you how your tax is worked out.

HOW DOES THE TAX SYSTEM WORK?

Getting to grips with the tax system is not difficult. Tax is levied on all your sources of income, whether it comes from earnings or investments. Most people pay tax at the basic rate which currently stands at 27 per cent. But you don't pay tax on all your income. You are allowed to deduct certain allowances and outgoings from it. This gives you a figure for taxable income which the Inland Revenue uses for working out your tax bill.

To take the simplest example. You are a single person with no taxable investment income and you earn £10,000 in the 1987–88 tax year. To work out your taxable income you subtract the Single Person's Personal Allowance of £2,425 from your income of £10,000. This gives a figure for taxable income of £7,575. Apply the basic rate of tax of 27 per cent to this figure and you arrive at a tax bill of £2,045 for the year.

From this you see that the most important part of working out your tax bill is checking whether you have claimed all the allowances and outgoings to which you are entitled.

Each year at the budget the Government adjusts the threshold at which people pay tax. This is done by increasing the level of personal tax allowances. The Chancellor of the Exchequer is required by law to increase the most important tax allowances by at least the rate of inflation. Below is a list of the personal tax allowances, who can claim them and how much they were worth in the 1987–88 tax year.

PERSONAL TAX ALLOWANCES 1987–88

Single Person's Personal Allowance (£2,425). You claim this allowance if you are single or divorced.

Married Man's Personal Allowance (£3,795). Only married men can claim this allowance (but see pages 56 and 57).

Wife's Earned Income Allowance (£2,425). You must claim this allowance once you are married. You can only set it against earned income, not investment income.

Additional Personal Allowance (£1,370). This allowance makes up the difference between the Married Man's Personal Allowance and the lower Single Person's Personal Allowance. You can claim this allowance if you are single and have a child living with you. If the child is not your own, he or she must be financially dependent on you. A married man can get this allowance if his wife is incapacitated during the entire tax year.

Age Allowance (Single person £2,960, married £4,675). You can claim this allowance if you or your husband are 65 or over. The allowance replaces the Single Person's and Married Man's Personal Allowances. If your income is above £9,800 (this figure changes every year) your age allowance is reduced on a sliding scale. But it can never be less than the Single Person's or Married Man's Personal Allowances. Age Allowance is increased for pensioners over 80 to £3,070 for single people and £4,845 for married men.

Widow's Bereavement Allowance (£1,370). This allowance is also intended to make up the difference between the Married Man's and the Single Person's Personal Allowance. You claim it in the year your husband dies and the following year.

Housekeeper Allowance (£100). Widows and widowers get this allowance if they have someone living with them and acting as a housekeeper.

Dependent Relative Allowance (£145). If you are single, widowed, divorced or taxed separately from your husband you can get this allowance for each relative you support financially. The relative doesn't have to live with you, but they must be permanently ill, disabled or over 65. And to get the full allowance they must earn less than the State basic old age pension. Men can only claim an allowance of £100.

Allowance for a Son or Daughter on Whose Services You Depend (£55). You can get this allowance if you are permanently ill, disabled or over 65 and you maintain a son or daughter who looks after you.

Blind Person's Allowance (£540). If you or your husband are registered blind with your local authority, you can get this allowance.

For the Inland Revenue leaflet on allowances ask for IR22.

HOW TO CHECK YOUR NOTICE OF CODING

If you work for just one employer and your only investment income is from a bank or building society, your Notice of Coding is your most important tax document. You probably won't see a tax return from one year to the next. Although if you feel the urge to fill one in, you can always ask your tax office to send you one. If your circumstances don't change from year to year, you may not see a fresh Notice of Coding every year either. The Notice of Coding shows you how your tax code is worked out. Your employer uses your tax code to work out how much tax to take off your pay through the PAYE system. If your tax code is correct, you are unlikely to be paying too much tax.

Check you are claiming all the allowances and outgoings to which you are entitled. Don't credit the Inland Revenue with the power to read your mind. If you don't tell them when your life changes, no one else will.

Remember to tell them when you:

- Get married, divorced or widowed.
- Have a child while single.
- Take out a loan which qualifies for tax relief.

Most loans and mortgages you take out to buy or improve the home you live in qualify for tax relief. Most mortgage repayments now have the basic rate of tax taken off at source under the MIRAS scheme. Unless you are a higher-rate taxpayer, these loans no longer feature on the Notice of Coding. If, on the other hand, your mortgage is outside the scope of MIRAS, or you have a home improvement loan, get your Notice of Coding altered so you pick up the tax relief through your pay packet.

You get tax relief on your mortgage interest payments at your top rate of tax. If you pay your mortgage through MIRAS you are only getting tax relief at the basic rate. To get the relief at higher rates of tax, an adjustment is made to your Notice of Coding.

The Notice of Coding is a cunning document. The tax people can also use it to collect your unpaid taxes. If you have investment income which isn't taxed before you get it, or your employer hands out fringe benefits, the Inland Revenue may decide to tax them through your pay packet rather than send you a tax bill at the end of the year. The main sources of untaxed investment income are certain National Savings schemes, especially the Investment Account, and Government stocks bought through National Savings.

Basic-rate taxpayers have no extra tax to pay on the income they get from most bank and building society savings schemes, or on the dividend income from company shares and unit trusts – the tax is already taken off when you get it. If you pay higher-rate tax, on the other hand, you do have extra to pay and the Inland Revenue may want to collect it by adjusting your tax code.

The Inland Revenue can now calculate your tax code. They do this by adding up all your allowances and outgoings, less any deductions or adjustments. From this total they knock off the last number and add a code letter. This normally gives you a code of three numbers and one letter.

There are five possible code letters:

- **L** stands for 'lower' and indicates you are claiming the Single Person's or Wife's Earned Income Allowance.

- **H** stands for 'higher'. This letter shows you are claiming the Married Man's Personal Allowance or the Additional Personal Allowance on top of the Single Person's Personal Allowance.

- **P** is the letter you get if you claim the Single Person's Age Allowance.

- **V** is the letter for the Married Man's Age Allowance.

- **T** is the all-purpose letter which is used in odd cases or where you don't want your employer to guess your personal circumstances. Write to your tax office if you want it.

On pages 64 and 65 you can see how a Notice of Coding works. I have taken as my example a woman who earns £18,000 a year with a company car. She is single but has a small daughter who lives with her and who she supports. She has various

NOTICE OF CODING

Inland Revenue
PAYE

Please use this reference if you write or call. It will help to avoid delay.

Issued by H.M. Inspector of Taxes

Date ....

Notice of coding

Year to 5 April 198

Code *See form P3* 303 H

About this notice of coding

This notice cancels any previous notice of coding for the above year. It shows overleaf the allowances which make up your code.

Your employer or paying officer will use this code to deduct or refund the right amount of tax under PAYE during the above year.

If this notice is issued after 5 April this code will be used as soon as possible.

What you need to do

- Check that the allowances and code shown on this form are correct. An "allowance" is an amount of your income on which you do not pay tax. If you think the allowances or code are wrong, please let me know and return this form. If we cannot agree you have the right of appeal.
- Otherwise keep this form in case you need to refer to it again.

If your personal circumstances change

- Please tell me at once, because your code has been based on your circumstances as known at the time of coding.
- Tell me if you change your address.

P2

A form P3 (PAYE coding guide) is enclosed or was sent to you with a previous notice of coding

How your PAYE code is calculated

Expenses		....
Death and Superannuation Benefits		....
Interest unless payable net of tax		....
Personal allowance		2,335
Age allowance (estimated total income £............)		....
Wife's earned income allowance		....
Additional personal allowance		1,320
Dependent relative allowance		....
Widow's bereavement allowance...		....
....		....
....		
Total allowances		3,655
Less allowances given against other income		
Untaxed interest...	100	
Occupational pensions	....	
State pension/benefits	....	
Benefits (car)	525	625
Net allowances		3,030
Less adjustments for		
....		
....		
Tax unpaid for earlier years 198 -8 £............ equivalent to a deduction of	....	
198 -8 (estimated £............) equivalent to a deduction of		
Allowances given against pay etc.		3,030

Your code is shown overleaf

Printed for HMSO by A. Pettitt Ltd 9 86 8976678

investments, but with the exception of a National Savings Investment Account all the other investment income she receives is taxed before she gets it. This is the Notice of Coding she received in January 1987 for the 1987–88 tax year. It is based on the previous year's tax allowances, but these are automatically adjusted if there is any change in the budget.

Under 'Personal Allowance' the Inland Revenue enter a figure of £2,335, which is her Single Person's Personal Allowance. Lower down under 'Additional personal allowance' they enter £1,320, which she is entitled to claim for her daughter. This gives a figure for 'Total allowances' of £3,655.

In the next section they enter a figure of £100 for 'Untaxed interest'. This is roughly what she expects to receive in the tax year just ending, so she doesn't bother to question the amount.

You only pay tax on your company fringe benefits if you earn above a certain amount (the figure was £8,500 in the 1987–88 tax year). She earns more than this and must pay tax on her company car. This is assessed on a sliding scale depending on the age and original cost of the car. In her case the taxable benefit is assessed at £525 a year.

This adjustment is written in separately. It gives a total figure for deductions of £625 a year. This is deducted from her personal allowances to give a final figure for 'Allowances given against pay' of £3,030. Her tax code is 303H, which is £3,030 less the last number plus the suffix H because she is claiming the Additional Personal Allowance as well as the Single Person's Personal Allowance.

FILLING IN YOUR TAX RETURN

You only have to fill in a tax return if you, or your husband's, finances are relatively complicated. If you are married and want to fill in your own tax return you must either opt for Separate Assessment or separate taxation. Otherwise you enter your information on your husband's tax return. There are three types of tax return. You are most likely to get form P1, but if you pay higher-rate tax or have large amounts of investment income you get form 11P. If you are self-employed you get form 11.

The tax return does several things. Take the example of the 1987–88 tax return which went out in the spring of 1987.

- If you are an employee it allows the Inland Revenue to check the tax you paid through PAYE in the tax year just ending. If you haven't paid enough they send you a bill, or make an adjustment to your Notice of Coding. If they owe you money, they send you a refund or make an adjustment to your Notice of Coding.

- If you are self-employed it allows the Inland Revenue to check your accounts. These don't have to coincide with the tax year. You can choose to run your accounts from any date in the year. In fact, it is to your advantage to have your accounting year run from near the beginning of a tax year. The Inland Revenue want to see the accounts whose year end fell during the tax year just ending. So if your accounts run from June to June, you file your accounts for the period June 1985 – June 1986 with your 1987–88 Tax Return.

- You use your Tax Return to let the Inland Revenue know which allowances you are claiming for the tax year just beginning. If you are an employee and pay tax through PAYE, your tax office can send you a new Notice of Coding, if necessary.

- If you are an active investor or buy and sell collectable items, you may have to pay Capital Gains Tax.

You pay income tax on all your sources of income, after deducting all the allowances and outgoings to which you are entitled. Most people pay income tax at the basic rate only. This currently stands at 27 per cent.

Higher-rate tax is charged on a sliding scale. It is only charged on the slice of income which falls within the appropriate tax band, so you don't pay your top rate of tax on all your income, just on a proportion of it.

In the 1987–88 tax year higher-rate tax started at £17,901.

The tax bands looked like this:

£17,901 and £20,400	40 per cent
£20,401 and £25,400	45 per cent

£25,401 and £33,300	50 per cent
£33,301 and £41,200	55 per cent
£41,201 and above	60 per cent

If the sight of one of those fat brown envelopes brings on a panic attack, fight the urge to throw it in the bin. If you work for an employer and pay your tax through PAYE, filling in your tax return is a job which shouldn't take more than half an hour.

To help you avoid a nervous breakdown, here are a few of the tricks of the trade:

- When you enter your earnings remember to deduct any payments you made into your workplace pension scheme. If it is a statutory scheme or approved by the Inland Revenue (they almost always are) these payments are tax-free and the Inland Revenue doesn't want to know about them. Get the figure from your P.60, which your employer should send you soon after the end of the tax year – the figure usually excludes any pension contributions.

- The same applies to profit-related pay. Some companies link a proportion of their employees' pay to profits. Since April 1987, you don't pay tax on half of any pay which is profit-related, and you don't need to declare the amount which is tax-free. Again the figure will not appear on your P.60.

- Fringe benefits are taxable if you are classified as higher paid (earning more than £8,500 in the 1987–88 tax year). If you have a company car there is a sliding scale for working out the value of the benefit. It varies with the size and age of the car and how much you use it for business. For example if your company car is under four years old, has an engine capacity of less than 1,400 cc and cost no more than £19,250 to buy, the car is said to be worth an extra £525 a year to you. Enter this amount on your tax return.

- Since 6 April 1985, if your child is cared for in a nursery provided by your employer, you pay tax on the benefit if you fall into the higher-paid category.

- You don't have to enter interest from tax-free investments such as National Savings Certificates, Yearly Plan and Save-As-You-Earn, or winnings from Premium Bonds.

○ You must enter the interest you get from banks and building societies even though they are taxed at source and you won't have any extra tax to pay unless you are a higher-rate taxpayer.

○ If you invest in company shares or unit trusts, keep your dividend statements. You need them for filling in your tax return. Enter the amount you received and the tax credit, which is the amount already taken off for tax.

○ There is a separate section for income which isn't taxed when you get it. This is where you enter any income from Government stocks bought through the Post Office and registered on the National Savings Stock Register (see Chapter 11).

○ If you work for an employer, there are very few expenses which you can claim against tax. For example, if you have to dress smartly for your job you don't get tax relief on your clothes, even on those you never wear outside work. And if you have children, and pay for them to be looked after while you are at work, you can't claim the cost of child care. But if you use your own car in your work (but not for travelling to and from work) you can claim a proportion of the cost of running your car. If your employer pays you a mileage allowance but this doesn't cover the full cost, you can claim the shortfall. If it's part of your contract of employment that you work at least some of the time from home you may be able to claim a proportion of your household expenditure.

○ You can claim tax relief on money you borrow to improve the house you own, so long as you remain below the £30,000 limit for mortgage interest relief.

The tax system has a soft spot for those who work for themselves. Apart from anything else, you can quite legitimately arrange to pay your tax bill nearly two years in arrears. And there are special tax allowances to help you buy equipment for your business, anything from telephones to machine tools.

- If you are self-employed, prepare proper accounts. Unless you are running a business which employs people, you can probably compile these yourself without the help of an accountant.

- Make sure you claim all your expenses. Things like raw materials, rent and wages are obvious. But if you work from home don't forget to claim a proportion of your household bills – rent, heating, lighting, maintenance, cleaning, and insurance. You can claim part of your rates bill too, but the Inland Revenue may argue that you are using a proportion of your house exclusively for business and ask for some Capital Gains Tax when you sell your house. If you have a car, claim a proportion of the cost of running it.

- Each time you buy something large for your business – it could be a computer, a car, or office furniture – your tax office helps foot the bill with their system of Capital Allowances. In the first year, you claim up to 25 per cent of the cost. In the following years you claim up to 25 per cent of the written-down value of the item. This is what you paid for the item less the accumulated Capital Allowances already claimed.

CHECKING YOUR TAX

A good time to check you have paid the correct amount of tax is when your employer sends you your P.60, which they should do soon after the end of the tax year. You may find the figure on your P.60 doesn't tally with the figure for accumulated pay on the year's final payslip. This is usually because the income figure on the P.60 is entered after deducting pension fund contributions and any tax-free profit-related pay.

If you pay basic-rate tax you can probably check your tax on the back of an envelope. Higher-rate taxpayers should arm themselves with a calculator.

If you are a basic-rate taxpayer, start by adding up all your sources of income. Your income from employment is the figure after deducting pension contributions and any tax-free profit-related pay. Don't forget fringe benefits and any investment income which is paid gross. You can ignore the income from tax-free investments and where the income is taxed at source. This is your total income.

From the figure for total income deduct all the allowances and outgoings to which you are entitled. If you pay your mortgage under the MIRAS system, you don't need to bring it into the calculation.

Now you know your taxable income you can work out how much tax you should have paid.

If you are a higher-rate taxpayer there are added complications. You pay extra tax on your investment income and if you pay your mortgage through MIRAS the Inland Revenue owe you extra tax relief.

So to calculate your tax bill you need to make certain adjustments. First gross up any investment income taxed at source. If tax is at 27 per cent you do this by dividing the net amount you received by 0.73. This gives you the amount of income you would have received if no tax had been deducted. Add this figure to your total income.

Next ask your bank or building society for the gross amount of interest you paid on the first £30,000 of your mortgage and add this to the figure for allowances and outgoings.

You are now in a position to work out your taxable income, and how much tax you should pay. However, there are still a couple of further adjustments to be made. You have already paid basic-rate tax on any investment income taxed at source, so remember to deduct these payments from the amount of tax you owe. Conversely, if you pay your mortgage through MIRAS you have already received tax relief at the basic rate and must add this back to your tax bill. With basic-rate tax at 27 per cent, work this out by multiplying your interest payment by 0.27.

A **Notice of Assessment** is likely to be the most daunting tax document you ever receive. If you regularly fill in a tax return, pay higher-rate tax or work for yourself, you must grapple with one of these every year.

If you do get one every year, wait for it to arrive before you check your tax bill. If you have several different sources of earned income – say you work for an employer and do freelance work in your free time – you may get more than one Notice of Assessment. The one covering your self-employed earnings is sent with a bill.

Notices of Assessment are notoriously difficult to understand, especially if you pay higher-rate tax. Tricky areas such as investment income taxed at source, and mortgage interest relief are worked out by adjusting the threshold at which you start paying higher-rate tax. Don't spend too long trying to understand the logic. If you find it too baffling, ring up your tax office and ask them to explain it.

ARGUING WITH THE INLAND REVENUE

If you think the Inland Revenue owes you money, write to your tax office – your employer can give you the address – telling them why. They will probably send you a tax return to fill in. But at least you have taken the first step towards getting a refund.

Women who stop work to have a baby often forget to claim a tax refund. If you pay tax through PAYE and stop work before the end of the tax year, you are almost certainly owed a rebate. Don't forget to claim it. Depending on when you stop work, it can be worth hundreds of pounds.

If you find you owe the Inland Revenue money because you have failed to let them know of some source of income, again you must write and explain what has happened. If the Inland Revenue have made the mistake, just keep quiet. There is just a chance they may never notice. If they do discover their error, you may be let off paying some of the tax you owe.

You can appeal against a Notice of Assessment. You must lodge your appeal within 30 days of the date on the assessment, unless you have a good excuse – like you were on holiday. With tax assessments on freelance or self-employed earnings, if you don't want to pay your tax bill immediately you must give your reasons for appealing and ask for a postponement.

Appeals are either heard by the General Commissioners or the Special Commissioners. If you fight your own case it costs you nothing. However, it's normally possible to argue it out with your tax office before the case actually reaches the Commissioners. If you can't agree, Inland Revenue leaflet IR37 tells you how to use the appeal system.

[1] Halifax Building Society.

£££

5
Becoming a woman of property

The British are obsessed with owning their own homes. There is hardly any other country in the developed world which puts such a high premium on owning the roof over its head. So much so that home ownership has risen from 30 per cent in 1951 to 62 per cent at the end of 1985[1].

It is of course hardly surprising. Any Government which is prepared to give away £2.5 billion a year in tax relief to people buying their own homes can't be surprised that home ownership is the nation's favourite method of creating personal wealth[2]. It's so popular that nearly two fifths of the nation's personal wealth is held in the form of bricks and mortar[3]. No other type of investment comes anywhere near it.

But you can't con people that easily. If it didn't make financial sense people wouldn't do it. And for most people, buying their own home has been a cast iron, copper-bottomed investment. Since the Second World War, house prices have consistently risen faster than inflation. A couple starting their married life 30 years ago in 1957 could have bought a semi-detached house in the South East for around £2,500. Today that house would be worth around £52,250 – a rise of more than 20 times. The rate of inflation rose by just over eight times over the same period.

Even when inflation raged at its most rampant during the three years between 1974 and 1976, when prices in the shops rose by 72 per cent, house prices more than managed to keep pace.

Of course those were the days of hyperinflation when mortgaging yourself to the hilt made sound financial sense. And even when mortgage rates reached 15 per cent in 1979, tax relief reduced that to 10 per cent. And when you compared it with an inflation rate which at one point in 1975 nearly touched 27 per cent, you were better off borrowing money than saving it. The advice was to borrow today, because tomorrow's pay rise would soon reduce the pain of those hefty mortgage repayments.

The picture today is by no means so cut and dried. In spite of the fierce competition between the banks and building societies, cheap mortgages are a thing of the past. It now costs around 5 per cent a year in real terms to borrow money to buy a house. The mortgage rate seems to fluctuate between 10 and 13 per cent. Tax relief reduces the rate to between 7 and 10 per cent. Adjusted for inflation the real cost of borrowing is around 5 per cent a year. If you borrowed most of the purchase price of your house, its value must rise each year by at least this amount if you aren't to lose money.

Whether it does or not depends a lot on where you happen to live. If you owned a house anywhere in the South East, where the demand for houses and the amount of money chasing them seems inexhaustible, your house probably increased in value by a least a fifth during 1986[4].

The same is not true for the rest of the country. The worst hit area, Scotland, saw increases of less than five per cent in 1986[4]. And in the once booming oil town of Aberdeen, house prices have actually fallen. In some cases so sharply that home owners are selling for less than they owe on their mortgages.

High levels of unemployment have also left their mark. The building societies repossessed 20,550 homes in 1986, eight times more than in 1979[5]. The level of repossession is small when set against the six million people with a building society mortgage. Nonetheless, each case represents a personal tragedy, and one which will continue to dog that family for many years, making it difficult for them to borrow money in the future.

So don't take it as read, that becoming a proud home owner is necessarily the best way to build wealth. Always think carefully before accepting any investment orthodoxy. Look at where you are planning to live. Is the area in demand, or are employment prospects depressing property prices? Two of the largest building societies, the Halifax and the Nationwide, produce regional statistics on house prices. Ask them what is happening to house prices in your area, and how they have moved in the last five years or so.

If you do rent and you like where you live, think carefully before you rush into house purchase. Don't be in any hurry to give up a cheap rent and a protected tenancy.

Remember too that money tied up in houses is not easily turned into ready money. You may be able to get your hands on some of the profit when you move house, and you may be able to use it as security when you borrow money. But unless you decide to sell up and return to rented accommodation, most people don't realise their property profits until they move to a smaller house at or near retirement. If you think you want money before then, don't put all your wealth-building eggs into the house-buying basket.

GETTING A MORTGAGE

You can ask any bank or building society for a mortgage; you don't necessarily have to be saving with them. But if there are mortgage queues, you stand a better chance of getting your mortgage if you do (see page 25).

Nor are the banks and the buildings societies the only place to get a mortgage. In the last couple of years a handful of insurance companies such as Allied Dunbar, Abbey Life, Commercial Union, Crown Life, Eagle Star, Guardian Royal Exchange, the Pearl and the Prudential have all started lending for house purchase.

There is also a new breed of lenders, such as the Mortgage Corporation and National Home Loans. These mortgage companies raise their mortgage funds by parcelling together a group of mortgages into a kind of bond which is then sold to the public.

But whoever you go to, the amount you can borrow still depends on the same two factors:

- The lender's valuation of the property.

○ Your ability to repay the mortgage.

Most lenders advance up to 80 per cent of their valuation of the property (this may be different from the purchase price) as a matter of course. You may persuade them to give you more. But you will have to take out a **mortgage guarantee policy**. This way your lender isn't out of pocket if you can't keep up your mortgage repayments and your house is sold for less than you borrowed.

If you are buying on your own, most lenders let you borrow between two and half and three times your annual salary. If you are self-employed you normally have to produce three years' audited accounts.

If you are borrowing with someone else, whether it's a husband, lover or girl friend, you can usually borrow between two and a half times and three times the larger salary, plus the lesser salary. Some lenders also consider lending between two and two and a half times the joint salaries, if this produces a larger figure.

So if you earn £15,000 a year, and the girl friend you want to share with earns £12,000 you may be able to borrow up to £67,500, or two and a half times your joint salaries of £27,000. This is more than three times the higher salary plus the lower salary which produces a mortgage of £57,000.

Buying a house or flat with a group of people is often the only chance young people in their early twenties have of owning the roof over their head, especially in the South East. All the big building societies and banks lend to people who want to share, although some like the Woolwich won't take on more than three people.

Most lend up to three times the highest salary plus one of everyone else's salary. These are not hard and fast rules and depend on circumstances. If you think you might want to buy somewhere to share, don't invest with any building society until you know roughly how much they would lend you.

But as trainee solicitor Jennifer Williams discovered, these multiples are often not generous enough when you try and buy a flat in London. She and two friends, another trainee solicitor and a Lieutenant in the Navy, decided to buy a property to share. They found a flat they all liked in Clapham, South London. Their problems only began when they tried to get a mortgage.

The normal lending criteria left them far short of the money they needed to buy the flat. None of the big banks or building societies were prepared to allow for the fact that Jennifer and her friend's salaries would double the following year once they were fully trained.

Disaster followed disaster. A mortgage broker fixed them up with a small building society, and a top up loan from an insurance company. The deal then fell through after contracts were signed and deposits exchanged when the insurance company pulled out. They faced losing their deposit.

They only managed to salvage the situation when Jennifer remembered she had a friend who worked for a Canadian bank. It turned out that they were prepared to lend two and a half times the two largest salaries and base the calculation on their salaries as qualified solicitors. What's more, the mortgage came through within 48 hours.

The big building societies and banks do seem to be making it very difficult for young people to buy property jointly. There are of course problems: like what do you do when one person wants to move and get their money out? And what happens when people fall out? It is definitely a good idea to have a formal legal agreement between you if you do decide to share. But having said that, one would think that flat sharers were a safer lending proposition than couples, where the advent of a family can cause a big drop in joint incomes.

Ten years ago many building societies were still extremely hide-bound by convention. Some were discriminating against women, especially in joint applications for mortgages where the wife earned more than her husband. In 1978 the Equal Opportunities Commission reported that more than one in three building society branches offered such couples lower mortgages than those where the husband earned the higher salary.

The five largest societies, Halifax, Abbey National, Nationwide, Leeds and Woolwich, and the four big clearing banks all say there is now no discrimination against women so long as the sums added up and there are high enough earnings to meet the mortgage repayments. But it is worth remembering that where a wife earns more than her husband it is illegal under the Sex Discrimination Act 1975 for any lender to refuse to base the mortgage advance on the wife's earnings.

Not that everything is plain sailing. You may still have problems raising money if you want to improve a run-down property, buy a freehold flat (i.e. a flat with the freehold for the whole building), or a property with a sitting tenant. Mortgages on properties which are both business and residential such as pubs and guest houses are also tricky. And you may well be shown the door if you are self-employed and don't have a three-year earnings record to show for it.

Whatever you are trying to buy, if all the major banks and building societies turn you down, try a mortgage broker. They specialise in finding money for people who can't raise it from conventional sources. They don't necessarily resort to second-line banks and finance houses. They are just as likely to get you the money from a small regional building society you have never heard of.

Wherever it comes from, expect to pay a higher rate of interest than on a normal mortgage. Mortgage brokers earn their living from the commission they get from insurance companies, so you will be sold an insurance-linked mortgage. If you really don't want such a mortgage, insist on a repayment mortgage and offer the broker a fee for his service instead.

WHICH TYPE OF MORTGAGE?

There are three types of mortgage:

- The repayment mortgage.
- The insurance-linked or endowment mortgage.
- The pension mortgage.

When you take out a **repayment mortgage**, each monthly payment contains an element of interest and an element of capital repayment. In the early years you pay mostly interest. At the end of the mortgage term you repay mostly capital.

Most people now pay their mortgage payments net of basic-rate tax under MIRAS, which stands for Mortgage Interest Relief at Source. Under MIRAS your repayments are normally arranged so they stay the same throughout the mortgage term, only changing with interest rates. This is known as the constant net repayment method.

This isn't the case for loans which fall outside the scope of MIRAS. Here the net cost of your mortgage, after tax relief, rises as the interest element in each payment falls. You claim your tax relief through your tax code and the amount you get each year declines over the mortgage term.

There is no element of life insurance with a repayment mortgage (some banks insist you take it out). If people depend on you to pay the mortgage, make sure there is enough money to repay it if you die early. The cheapest way of doing this is with a **mortgage protection policy**. A good value company such as Equitable Life charges a woman age 30 a monthly premium of £2.30 to cover a mortgage of £30,000 over 25 years, with the mortgage rate at 11.25 per cent. A woman age 40 with the same mortgage but over 20 years would be charged £4.22 a month.

If you are single with no dependants a mortgage protection policy is a waste of money. Better to put the money into a savings scheme which directly benefits you.

There are several types of **insurance-linked** or **endowment mortgages**. With all of them the principle is the same. You take out a mortgage in the normal way from a bank or a building society. But instead of repaying the loan bit by bit throughout the mortgage term, you only pay the interest. You repay the mortgage out of the proceeds of an insurance policy. The policy usually pays out more than you need to repay the mortgage, so you get a lump sum as well to spend as you please. This is the big advantage insurance mortgages have over straight repayment mortgages.

The cheapest type is the **low-cost endowment**. These policies are specially designed to use with mortgages. The premiums are kept low, but the lump sum is modest.

Non-profit endowment policies pay out the exact amount needed to repay the mortgage. There is no particular advantage over a straight repayment mortgage.

With-profits endowment policies are expensive, but you get a larger lump sum than with a low-cost policy.

Unit-linked policies work more like a unit trust regular savings plan. Banks and building societies have now come to terms with unit-linked policies, although apparently few people choose them. They tend to perform better than low-cost endowment policies, but because the value of the policy is linked to units in a fund there is actually no guarantee the money will be there when the mortgage term is up. They can be more flexible than a low-cost endowment. For example, you can cash in the policy as soon as the units are worth the amount needed to repay the mortgage without penalty.

The self-employed or anyone without a company pension scheme can take out a **pension mortgage**. It works in the same way as an insurance-linked mortgage, but instead of using a life insurance policy to repay the mortgage you use the proceeds of a self-employed pension plan. You save tax too. Within certain limits you get tax-relief on payments into an approved self-employed pension scheme.

Choosing the best mortgage to go for is a nightmare. Your first task is to find out how much your mortgage is going to cost you. You need to know:

- The quoted interest rate.
- The true rate of interest or APR (Annual Percentage Rate).
- The monthly repayments.

Comparing mortgage interest rates doesn't always tell the full story. The banks and the building societies have different ways of charging interest. If you ask for the true rate of interest (or APR) you can compare interest rates more accurately. For example, you may find that a quoted interest rate from a building society of, say, 12 per cent is actually more expensive than a bank's quoted rate of 12¼ per cent.

You normally pay less each month with a repayment mortgage than with a low-cost endowment mortgage. The latter is only cheaper if the mortgage rate falls below 10 per cent. In the last five years the lowest the mortgage rate has fallen to is 10 per cent between November 1982 and June 1983. Repayment mortgages remain slightly cheaper, even when you add on the cost of a mortgage protection policy.

With the mortgage rate at 11.25 per cent (as it was at the time of writing), a 30-year-old woman taking out a 25-year mortgage for £30,000 under MIRAS pays £238.47 a month for a repayment mortgage with the Nationwide building society, plus another £2.30 a month for a mortgage protection policy, making a total of £240.77 a month.

A low-cost endowment policy with Equitable Life costs her £245.41 a month; with the insurance premium costing £40.10 a month; the interest on the mortgage £205.31 a month. With the repayment mortgage there is no lump sum at the end of the mortgage term. Equitable Life estimates that her low-cost endowment policy will be worth £42,648 in 25 years' time. She uses £30,000 to repay her mortgage which leaves her a lump sum of £12,648.

But nothing about these figures is guaranteed. The size of your lump sum could be smaller, it could be larger. It all depends on the future profits of your insurance company and the level of bonuses they allocate to your policy. Remember too, sums which look like fortunes today, can appear quite modest in 25 years' time when inflation has done its work. So take those insurance company projections with a big pinch of salt.

Repayment mortgages are more flexible than endowment mortgages. With a repayment mortgage, if interest rates go up and you can't afford to pay the extra you can ask your bank or building society to extend the term of the loan. With insurance-linked mortgages you can't do this; you are locked into the term of the policy.

There may be circumstances in which you need to cash in your insurance-linked mortgage. If you do this in the first 10 years, you are unlikely to get all your premiums back.

Avoid insurance-linked mortgages if:

- You are mortgaged to the hilt. A sudden increase in interest rates could leave you short of money.

- There is any chance you might want to cash in an insurance-linked mortgage in the first ten years. This could happen for a variety of reasons. You might want to live abroad. If you are sharing with someone, you might want to go your separate ways.

If you get married, you and your husband might want to organise your mortgage differently. As a general rule, single women should avoid insurance-linked mortgages.

HOME OWNERSHIP AND THE LAW

Make sure you understand the difference between a **joint tenancy** and **tenants-in-common.** If you buy property with someone else, or a group of people, you should have a legal agreement between you all.

If you are all contributing towards buying the property, make sure it's in everyone's name. You can then decide if you want to be joint tenants or tenants-in-common.

Under a joint tenancy, if someone dies, their share of the property automatically passes to the other owners. If you are a tenant-in-common, you have the right to leave your share of the property to whoever you like. If you die without making a will, your share is distributed according to the rules of intestacy. See Chapter Eight.

DOING UP OLD HOUSES

If your idea of fun is spending the next five years scraping off layers of Victorian varnish and picking out generations of paint from intricate mouldings you may be on your way to a lucrative new pastime.

But it isn't always easy getting started. The banks and building societies may agree to lend you the money to buy your run-down slum, but they won't give you all of it until certain basic work has been done. It's called a retention and it's a practice which puts many a would-be house improver right off the idea. Not only are you short of a crucial few thousand pounds to buy your house, but you haven't got the money to finance the improvements either.

Local authority improvement grants are useful if you can get them, but they are usually paid when you have finished doing up your house, so do nothing to solve your cash-flow crisis. The usual solution is to persuade your bank manager to give you a bridging loan. He may need convincing that you have the ability to get the work done before he lends you the money.

Women who manage to clamber over all these hurdles often discover a real talent for transforming grubby hovels into gracious homes, and then find they can't stop. Doing up your own home can be a profitable and tax-efficient way of earning your living, if you don't mind living with builders' rubble. You only get paid when you sell a house and move on to the next one, but if you have an eye for a bargain, the profits can be considerable. And they are tax-free.

You don't pay income tax or Capital Gains Tax when you buy and sell your principal residence. But just one word of caution. If you buy and sell too often, the Inland Revenue may try and classify you as a 'trader' and send you a bill for income tax on your property profits.

Theresa MacEwan has turned her passion for old houses into a lucrative livelihood. Theresa buys up run-down houses in Clapham, Wandsworth and Tooting, all increasingly fashionable areas of South London, and turns them into elegant family homes. She knew all the pitfalls after a spell working for a well-known interior designer, as well as doing up three houses for her own family.

Theresa always buys empty houses and she isn't in the flat conversion business – she likes the houses too much for that. But it's not all sentiment. Theresa explains: '*I operate in a quite small area of London. That way I know all the estate agents and I have a good feel for the market. I know every street and alleyway in my patch. An outsider might think that two streets look the same, but there can be quite subtle differences which can affect house prices. Without this kind of knowledge you can easily come a cropper in the residential property market.*'

House prices in these areas have been rising by at least 30 per cent a year for the last couple of years. But Theresa says she never takes this into account when she does her sums. If prices do rise while she is doing up the house, it's just an added bonus.

Theresa normally takes between four and six months to do up each house. But things can and do go wrong, although Theresa says she has never actually lost money on any of her houses: *'Time is the main fly in the ointment. Some houses take longer than you expect to finish. Others take three months to sell when you thought they would take a month. All my developments are financed with borrowed money, so the longer each house takes to do the higher my interest bill and the lower my profit.'*

[1] *Social Trends 17*, 1987, Chart 8.1.
[2] *Social Trends 16*, 1986, Chart 8.23.
[3] *Social Trends 17*, 1987, Chart 5.20.
[4] Halifax House Price Index, 1986, published by the Halifax Building Society.
[5] Building Societies Association.

£££

6
With my worldly goods I thee endow

Everyone loves a wedding. Witness the endless column inches of newspaper space which are devoted to our royal brides, with months of speculation on the cut of the dress and who is to be left off the invitation list. We lap up stories of hitherto unknown dress designers under siege from Japanese film crews camped in their front gardens. And we seem to have an insatiable appetite for the boarding school japes of our royal brides-to-be.

Weddings, but especially royal weddings, bring a little bit of romance into our humdrum lives. We hope some of that magic rubs off on us. So let's pause a moment before shattering that comforting illusion. The reality is, of course, different. Two in five marriages now end in divorce.

And once you have brushed off the confetti, shaken off the silken shoe, and come back down to earth, it's important to realise that at its most basic, marriage is no more than a legally binding contract between two people which imposes duties and responsibilities on both parties.

Contrary to popular belief, your husband does not have a duty to keep you in the style to which you are accustomed. In fact husbands and wives have a joint responsibility to maintain each other.

Nor are you under any obligation to take your husband's surname. You are quite free to continue using your unmarried name if you prefer. If you want to share a name with your husband but dislike the idea of taking his on principle, you are even free to choose an entirely different married name. In the last case you need to ask a solicitor to help you prepare documents which the banks, the Inland Revenue and the DHSS will accept.

PAYING THE BILLS

Who pays for what, can cause as many arguments as who does the washing up. Some couples like to keep their finances entirely separate. While others believe in total integration with both salaries going into a joint account, and all savings held jointly. Both extremes are unusual. Most couples now fall somewhere in the middle, and use a joint bank account for those household bills – electricity, gas, telephone and the weekly supermarket shop – for which they are both responsible. With a joint account, you are both responsible for any debts, and the bank has the right to recover the money from either of the account holders.

Jacquie and Richard Roberts are one of those rare couples who believe in total integration. Richard is a hospital consultant and Jacquie a university lecturer. They married in 1971 when Richard was still a medical student and Jacquie was earning around £900 a year. Richard says: '*We didn't have any money, just Jacquie's salary and my grant, so using a joint account and pooling all our spending didn't seem such a big deal, and we found it worked well.*'

The intervening years, and their increasing affluence has done nothing to change their opinion. Richard says: '*If either of us goes on a spending spree, we own up immediately.*'

In theory joint accounts are a great boon. In practice, they can be a headache. If you each have a cheque book, you may never know how much you have in your account. To avoid slipping into the red by accident, and running up bank charges, you may have to keep a hefty credit balance in the account – money which really ought to be earning interest elsewhere.

Jacquie and Richard keep their account in credit by using their Access credit card for as many purchases as possible and settling the bill with a single cheque when the account comes in, and making sure the bank sends them monthly rather than quarterly statements.

You can't hold credit cards jointly. But if you have a credit card, or are applying for one, you can arrange for your husband to have a card on your account, and vice versa. It's the main cardholder who is responsible for the debt, so if you have a spendthrift husband don't give him a card on your credit card account.

Banks and finance companies no longer automatically ask men to guarantee their wives' loans. However, it remains the case that women have more difficulty borrowing money than men. This is often because they can't offer the bank any security. The banks are no longer overtly discriminating against women, but there are still an awful lot of women who can't get loans unless they ask their husband to guarantee them.

The law can always throw up the odd curiosity which provides an insight into the way we used to live. For example, shops who know their legal onions may refuse to let you buy on tick. This is because a husband is responsible for his wife's household debts unless he can prove that he pays her sufficient housekeeping, and few shopkeepers are in a position to know that. Nowadays this is no more than a legal footnote. The whole notion of housekeeping allowances is archaic, and not many shops (even local shops) still run a slate.

MARRIAGE AND THE STATE

How marriage and the tax system work to women's disadvantage is explained in Chapter Four. Getting married can also affect your National Insurance contributions and your entitlement to State benefits.

If you work after you get married, you carry on paying National Insurance contributions just as you did when you were single. The change arises if you then stop work to look after young children or a sick or elderly relative. Instead of losing your right to all or some of your State benefits you now get something called **Home Responsibility Protection** (**HRP**). This effectively reduces the number of years you need to pay into the National Insurance scheme in order to qualify for State benefits.

You get HRP automatically if you get Child Benefit for a child under 16, or you are claiming social security in order to care for a sick or elderly relative. You need to claim it if you are looking after somebody who gets an Attendance Allowance or a Constant Attendance Allowance.

Some married women and widows still have the right to pay the old reduced National Insurance contributions, but you can only do this if you were already paying the lower stamp in 1977. For everyone else this facility was withdrawn when HRP was introduced. If you do still pay the reduced rate you can't get unemployment pay or your own State basic retirement pension.

And you lose the right to continue paying reduced contributions if you stop working for two or more consecutive years, or get divorced. Ask for National Insurance leaflet NI.1, 'Married women, your National Insurance position'.

If you opted to pay reduce contributions or there are big gaps in your National Insurance record, you can collect one of a number of Widows' Benefits and a State Basic Retirement Pension on your husband's contributions instead.

You can only claim this pension once your husband reaches 65, and you are over 60. It is only worth 60 per cent of the single person's pension and is added to your husband's pension. With a full contribution record you get your basic pension and any earnings-related pension when you reach 60. This counts as your income for tax purposes and the Married Woman's Earned Income Allowance can be set against it. The Inland Revenue treats any pension you claim on your husband's contributions as his income.

SPLITTING UP

It can be a hard job sustaining the romance of those early days of marriage when the dirty dishes stack up and the baby pours her second bowl of cereal on the floor. The women's magazines extol the virtues of yoga, or positive thinking, or gourmet cooking as the best way of injecting a little magic back into our jaded marriages.

Most of us don't have the time, and even if we did, successful marriages are probably more about learning to live with each other than striving for some romantic ideal. The divorce figures are a catalogue of broken dreams and false expectations. In 1985, 175,000 couples got divorced, and in nearly a quarter of these cases one or both of the partners had been divorced before[1].

The divorce rate has doubled since 1971 when more liberal divorce laws were introduced. You stand the best chance of staying married the longer you delay taking the plunge. The figures for 1984 show that in just over 78 per cent of divorces, the wife was less than 24 when she married. The divorce rate fell to less than 5 per cent for women who married between the ages of 30 and 34[2].

Divorce is a painful, soul-destroying process. You have to accept your feelings of failure or rejection. You worry about the children. And on top of all this you have to start haggling over the money.

However bitter you feel, try not to use money as the instrument of your revenge. The only people who usually gain from this sort of battle are the divorce lawyers. Try and get a voluntary agreement with your husband and then get the courts to agree to it.

Don't con yourself that you will be able to maintain your existing standard of living. It stands to reason that running two households is more expensive than running one. You must either accept you are going to have less to live on, or do something about improving your own finances. Spending the next 20 years waiting for your maintenance cheques is a sure recipe for poverty.

While you were married you may have decided to stay at home and look after young children. Now you are divorced you may decide to go back to work. Or you could start making plans for when the children are at school full-time. Going on a training course does great things for one's confidence. There are part-time courses which you can take a couple of mornings a week. Find one with a crèche.

THE DIVISION OF THE SPOILS

If your husband is being awkward, the courts have a rule of thumb for deciding how much you should get. It's only a rule of thumb, and with concepts like the 'clean break' – where the husband buys out the wife's right to maintenance for a lump sum – becoming more popular, it may not be relevant for many more years.

The courts look at the family's assets – in practice this is often the family house – and the family's total income, the husband's and the wife's. The wife is normally entitled to a share of the assets and maintenance of a third of the husband and wife's joint income. If you earn more than a third of the family's joint income, you may not get maintenance. Maintenance for the children is variable but is often set at around 7.5 per cent of the husband's income for each child.

In practice, of course, the courts decide cases individually and on their merits. Many young couples who divorce after just a couple of years of marriage, where both are still working and there are no children, agree to no maintenance. They part amicably, selling any jointly-held property and splitting the proceeds. They make the clean break.

In these circumstances there is very little point in a wife asking the courts for maintenance. If she gets anything it is only likely to be a nominal award, like 10p a year.

The welfare of children is rightly the first concern of the courts in a divorce case. This is where the knotty problem of the family home raises untold difficulties, especially where the home is the family's main asset, as is often the case. The courts are then torn between seeing a fair division of the family's assets and ensuring that the children have somewhere to live.

The best and neatest solution is usually to sell the family house and divide up the proceeds. But if the house isn't worth much or is heavily mortgaged, it's possible that neither husband or wife ends up with enough money to buy a new home.

If there are children and they are to live with their mother, there are several other possibilities, none of which is ideal.

○ The husband gives the family house to his wife and she agrees to take no maintenance for herself. The disadvantage of this approach is that the husband is often lumbered with mortgage payments on the house and he can't afford to buy another house for himself. But this is undoubtedly the best deal for women who have good prospects of earning their own living.

- The wife buys out her husband's share in the family house, either for a lump sum or by taking out a mortgage, and continues to get maintenance for herself from her husband. This is only an option if the wife can independently buy out her husband or has sufficient income to repay the mortgage.

- The house remains jointly owned, with the wife having the right to live in it (whether for ever, or until she remarries or the eldest child reaches 18 is for the courts to decide). This can obviously be very unfair on the husband who may have to continue paying a mortgage on his first wife's house with no prospect of being able to buy somewhere for himself.

In practice there is no blueprint and each divorce settlement is different. When Helen Yemm and her husband John divorced, Helen took a lump sum worth half the marital home, plus £1,000 to buy a replacement car. She took a year's maintenance of £5,000 to tide herself over until she got back on her feet, plus £2,000 a year for their son Henry.

Helen says: '*I probably could have got more, but I didn't want a fight. In the end I don't think my solicitor's bill came to more than £150. The one thing I now resent is having to go back to the court each time I want Henry's maintenance increased. There is never any argument about the amount, it's just that having to go back to court opens up old wounds. But our solicitors tell us there is no way that an element for inflation can be built into awards for maintenance.*'

HOW THE SPOILS ARE TAXED

Separation and divorce are painful enough without giving the taxman more than his fair share. Make sure you understand your tax position before you rush into any maintenance agreement. Hitting on the right formula can save hundreds of pounds. Even if you parted amicably, it is still worth making any maintenance agreement enforceable through the courts. And the way the tax system works, it may be better for most of your maintenance to be paid to your children.

To get the best deal you must consider:

- which type of maintenance payments – whether voluntary or enforceable – suits your circumstances best.
- your tax rate and your husband's.
- your children's tax position.
- whether you are getting all the mortgage tax relief which you are entitled to.

Voluntary maintenance payments are, as the name implies, an informal agreement between a parting couple for one to pay maintenance to the other. They have several disadvantages. The person receiving the maintenance has no security if the payments suddenly stop. And if you are the person paying the maintenance you can't claim tax relief on the payments. But the person receiving the payments has no tax to pay.

Voluntary payments only make financial sense if both husband and wife pay tax at the same rate, or in those rare cases where a wife gets maintenance from her husband but pays tax at a higher rate than him.

Even couples who part on friendly terms should opt for an enforceable maintenance agreement made under a court order. If you pay maintenance under a court order you get tax relief on the payments at your top rate of tax. If you are the person receiving maintenance, you are liable to income tax on the payments. So if the person paying the maintenance pays a higher rate of tax than the person receiving it, they save tax by going for an enforceable agreement.

If your maintenance payments are below a certain level – known as Small Maintenance Payments – the person paying maintenance hands over the gross amount and claims the tax relief from the Inland Revenue, either through PAYE or as a tax rebate. The person getting maintenance is then liable to income tax. Small maintenance payments are those of less than £48 a week or £208 a month, and £25 a week or £108 a month for a child, unless the order is made directly to the child in which case the higher limit applies.

So if you are responsible for paying maintenance of £30 a week and you are a basic-rate taxpayer, you pay £30 a week, and claim tax relief of 27p in the pound, or £8.10.

With larger maintenance payments the money is paid net of basic-rate tax. For example, if you are paying maintenance of £40 a week, you hand over £29.20, which is £40 less basic-rate of tax of 27p in the pound. You get any entitlement to higher-rate tax relief through PAYE or a tax rebate. If the person getting maintenance pays no tax, they can claim it back from the Inland Revenue. Basic-rate taxpayers have nothing more to pay. Higher-rate taxpayers get an extra bill worked out on the gross maintenance, i.e. on £40 not £29.20.

It is often worthwhile juggling your maintenance so that much of it is paid directly to your children. Children rarely have a large income (they commonly earn a few pounds each year from savings accounts) but just like everyone else they can claim a personal tax allowance. If both you and your husband pay tax at the same level, you save tax by having an amount roughly equal to the Child's Personal Allowance paid directly to the child. In the 1987–88 tax year the Single Person's Allowance was £2,425. Make sure the court order makes it clear that the maintenance is to be paid *to* the child and not *for* the child.

The rules on mortgage tax relief alter as soon as you separate. To begin with, you revert to the status of two single people which entitles you to mortgage tax relief on loans of up to £30,000 each. But unlike single people you can claim your tax relief on two properties, one for yourself and one for your former partner.

This is how it works: if you or your husband take out a mortgage to buy a new home, while continuing to pay some or all of the mortgage on the former family home, you are entitled to tax relief on both mortgages so long as the total doesn't exceed £30,000. This only works if you keep an interest in the former family home.

When the two mortgages amount to more than £30,000, work it so you can both claim mortgage tax relief. You can do this by increasing any maintenance payments. This is the way it commonly happens. The husband takes out a mortgage to buy himself a new home. He is still paying the mortgage on the former family home, and his two mortgages now come to more than £30,000. He therefore increases his maintenance payments to his wife. She takes over paying the mortgage on the family home and claims up to £30,000 mortgage tax relief in her own right.

The husband can claim tax relief on his maintenance payments in the normal way. And if the wife pays little or no tax, she can reclaim the tax already deducted from her maintenance payments. She automatically gets tax relief on her mortgage payments whether or not she pays tax so long as the mortgage is paid under MIRAS. If it isn't, she only gets tax relief if she is a taxpayer.

As you unstitch the seams of your marriage you will have a job keeping track of all the loose ends which crop up. To help you stay ahead, here is a check list of the most important points to remember.

○ If you don't want a divorce, but you no longer want to live with your husband, you can decide to separate instead. You can do this informally, but there are advantages if you ask a solicitor to draw up a deed of separation, or you can apply to the divorce courts for what is called a judicial separation. With a more formal separation, the Inland Revenue allows you to claim tax relief on any maintenance payments you make, and the payments can be enforced by the courts.

○ If you can't agree on maintenance you can apply to the courts. If you are separating, apply to the Magistrates Court. If you have already started divorce proceedings, you go to the County Court if the case is undefended, the High Court if the case is defended.

○ Your right to maintenance (but not your children's) ends when you get married again. You also risk losing it if you start living with someone. Maintenance for your children normally ends when they finish their full-time education.

○ You can apply for your maintenance and that of your children to be increased. By the same token your husband can apply for a reduction. It may be increased if your husband marries again. This is a major bone of contention with second wives who see no reason why they should effectively pay some of their income over to a first wife.

○ If your husband stops paying you maintenance, you can apply to the court and ask for the maintenance order to be enforced. If he still fails to pay up, the court can apply for an Attachment of Earnings Order. This way the maintenance is deducted from the husband's pay packet. If this isn't appropriate and the husband still refuses to pay, he can end up in prison.

○ If you are independently wealthy, earn more than your husband, or he has stayed at home to look after the children, he can apply to you for maintenance and a share of your assets. Member of Parliament, John Browne, even threatened to send his former wife to jail when she failed to pay him £49,000, the final instalment in a £270,000 divorce settlement.

○ Only the divorce courts can rule when there is a dispute as to how the family's assets are to be divided. If you are going for a judicial separation you may be at a disadvantage if the family home is in your husband's name. The courts may only give you a share if you can prove you made a financial contribution towards buying it.

○ There can be big tax advantages in the year you separate if you get your timing right. Taxpayers can claim the Wife's Earned Income Allowance up until they separate, and the Single Person's Personal Allowance for the rest of the tax year. In the 1987–88 tax year both tax allowances stood at £2,425, making a total possible tax allowance for that year of £4,850.

○ In the following tax years you claim the Single Person's Personal Allowance, and if your children live with you the Additional Personal Allowance worth £1,370 in the 1987–88 tax year. If there is more than one child, you can only claim one allowance, but if one or more of the children live some of the tax year with their father, he may also be able to claim the Additional Personal Allowance.

○ If you live with someone, but you aren't married, make sure you get your name put on the title deed of any house you own together. Unless you do, you may be denied your share of the house if you break up. To get anything you will then have to prove you made a financial contribution towards buying or improving the property. The Law Commission has proposed that unmarried couples should have similar right to married couples when they split up.

○ Watch out for joint accounts. Close them down as soon as you separate. Unless both signatures are required on the cheques, your husband can withdraw all the money, even run up an overdraft without your knowledge. If he then disappears, you are responsible for the overdraft.

○ Beware of Legal Aid. If your divorce is contested and you applied for Legal Aid, the Law Society can reclaim some of its costs from the proceeds of the sale of any property. You can put off the evil day by hanging on to the family house.

○ Check you are claiming all the benefits which you are entitled to. You may be able to get rent and rate rebates, Family Income Supplement, or Unemployment Benefit. If you get Child Benefit you can claim the One Parent Benefit of £4.70 a week.

[1] *Social Trends 17* 1987 Edition, Table 2.15.
[2] *Social Trends 16* 1986 Edition, Table 2.17.

7
The baby trap

Rachel Sanger and Steven Glynn are a couple who have decided to share the task of looking after their two-year-old daughter, Helen. They both work in computers; Rachel as a freelance computer consultant, Steven for a small software product company. They have organised their lives so that when Rachel is working Steven looks after Helen, and vice versa. Rachel works on Tuesday and Thursday, Steven on Monday, Wednesday and Friday.

Rachel believes that looking after children is important. She says: '*You change after you have children, and I believe men should experience those changes too. We didn't want our lives to be segregated: me responsible for child care, Steven for earning the money.*'

They both earn less money now, but Rachel says she hasn't really noticed it: '*We always knew this is what we would do once we had children so we never lived up to our limit.*'

Lucky Helen. Sad to say there are still very few families where both husband and wife decided to work less while their children are small. The women's movement has done many things – one thing it hasn't done much to change is the politics of family life. In this all-important matter we have somehow failed to persuade men to value our own work as highly as their own. And we must be doing a poor public relations job on motherhood that so few men want to join us as equals.

No one, except the most dyed-in-the-wool backwoodsman, denies us the right to personal ambition. It's just that we are expected to be ambitious *while* we bring up children, clean the house, and cook dinner parties for half a dozen business cronies of our husband. Men can bring their work home both physically and mentally. But some unwritten rule seems to preclude us from doing the same. Our work is not allowed to intrude on the family. It's the myth of superwoman and the sooner she is buried the better.

The reality, of course, is very different. Most women are constantly running to stand still, always juggling just one too many balls. The cost in terms of stress is enormous. So much so that many of us now opt out of marriage and motherhood entirely, as the marriage and birth rate figures demonstrate.

There were 702,000 new babies born in 1984, nearly 280,000 fewer than at the height of the sixties' baby boom in 1964. And the decline is even more dramatic than it appears at first sight. In 1964, for every 1,000 women of child-bearing age, 94 gave birth. Twenty years later that ratio had fallen to less than 60 babies for every 1,000 women of child-bearing age[1].

There has also been a rapid decline in the number of first marriages, from 369,000 in 1971 to 257,000 in 1985[2].

WHO LOOKS AFTER BABY?

It is probably obvious, but the younger your children and the more you have, the less likely you are to be working. Only 7 per cent of women with children under four work full time, although one in five do manage to work part-time. The figure rises as the age of the youngest child increases. So by the time the youngest child is between 11 and 15, 31 per cent of women are working full time, and 45 per cent part-time[3].

How many women with young children are forced to stay at home because they can't find anyone to look after their children at a price they can afford?

You are unlikely to get a place for your child at a local council nursery. Most nurseries have long waiting lists and entry is restricted to the really needy – children of working single parents or children at risk of abuse.

If you work part-time you may be lucky to have a husband or mother who can take your place while you go to work. The choice is then narrowed down to employing a nanny in your own home, using a childminder, or a private or workplace nursery.

The cost of a nanny can be prohibitive. At the top end of the market, a nanny working in London but not living in can ask for and get £120 a week in her pocket after tax and National Insurance.

Childminders – check they are registered with the local council – vary in quality. Your child is looked after with others in the childminder's own home. The charge for this varies between £20 and £40 a week depending on where you live.

Private nurseries are few and far between and there may be a long waiting list for the restricted number of places allocated to under-two-year-olds. It is quite common for private nurseries to charge between £50 and £75 a week.

Workplace nurseries – nurseries paid for by your employer – are even rarer, and a recent tax ruling is now hampering their development.

The majority of working women appear to rely on their families to look after their pre-school children while they are at work. A recent survey showed that 85 per cent of working women left their small children with their husband, mother or mother-in-law or another close relative when they went to work.

Childminders were used by around 16 per cent of working women with children below school age. Only 4 per cent employed a nanny. One per cent used private nurseries, the same were lucky enough to have a workplace nursery[4].

Once you have paid for someone to look after your children, paid your taxes, National Insurance and pension contributions, there is often precious little to be gained financially from working.

The tax system does little to encourage working women. Strictly speaking, the cost of child care as such is not an allowable expense which you can set against tax. And this is the same whether you are an employee or self-employed.

In 1978 drama critic, Catherine Itzin, appealed against the Inland Revenue ruling that she couldn't claim the cost of her child care as a business expense. Catherine Itzin is self-employed and anything she spends 'wholly and exclusively' in the course of her work is an allowable expense. Catherine argued that if she wasn't working she wouldn't need to pay someone to look after her children, therefore the expense must be allowable.

The Inland Revenue does allow self-employed women, but not employees, to claim some of the cost of child care against tax, but it must be dressed up as 'secretarial and research'. Catherine knew the score, but disliked the idea of subterfuge. She lost her case, and there has been no subsequent move from the Inland Revenue or the Government to ease the financial burden for women who work.

In fact, quite the reverse. If your child is at a nursery attached to your workplace and provided by your employer you could be taxed on the benefit (the difference between what it costs to provide the service and what you pay). Workplace nurseries are now classified as a fringe benefit. You can only escape paying tax on fringe benefits if you earn less than £8,500 a year.

However, there was a recent victory for working women with children who claim Family Income Supplement (FIS) – the payments which are made to low income families to bring their income up to subsistence level. One woman (who chooses to remain anonymous) argued she should be permitted to deduct the cost of child care from her income when working out her entitlement to FIS, and the local Social Security Tribunal accepted her argument. However, the DHSS have appealed.

MATERNITY BENEFITS

Babies used to come gift wrapped in a cheque for £25 from the DHSS. In the spring of 1987, the Government ran the gauntlet of women's anger when they scrapped the £25 Maternity Grant which almost every woman used to get whenever she had a baby. This was replaced for women on FIS or supplementary benefits with a payment of £80 from a new **Social Fund**.

At the same time the Government rolled Maternity Allowance (the flat-rate weekly payment paid by the State) and Maternity Pay (the earnings-related supplement paid by employers) into one new benefit, **Statutory Maternity Pay**, and made employers responsible for paying it.

Statutory Maternity Pay came into force for babies due on or after 21 June 1987. To get it you must have worked for the same employer for at least the six months up to your 26th week of pregnancy and be earning more than the amount at which you start paying National Insurance contributions – £39 a week in the 1987–88 tax year.

Statutory Maternity Pay is paid for 18 weeks (13 of the 18 weeks are paid from the sixth week before the baby is due, the other five weeks can be tacked on before or after, or a bit of both). You lose benefit if you continue working during the last six weeks of your pregnancy.

The amount of Statutory Maternity Pay you get depends on how long you have worked for your employer. If you were full-time for more than two years, or part-time (working more than eight hours a week) for more than five years, you get 90 per cent of your pay in the first six weeks.

It then falls to a lower flat-rate weekly amount. In the 1987–88 tax year, it was £32.85 a week. If you have only been in your job for between 26 weeks and two years, you get the lower flat-rate payments only. Remember, this is the minimum you are entitled to. Some employers treat pregnant women rather more generously. Making a claim is easier under the new system. All you need to do is tell your employer at least three weeks before you intend stopping work.

If you can't get Statutory Maternity Pay because you have recently changed jobs, or you are self-employed, you may be entitled to claim the new **Maternity Allowance** directly from the DHSS. It was worth £30.05 in the 1987–88 tax year, with additions for adult dependants.

When Statutory Maternity Pay runs out you can sign on as unemployed and collect unemployment pay. But you may be asked to prove that you are available for work. This could entail providing evidence of your child-care arrangements.

You also have the right to **maternity leave** if you have worked for your present employer for at least 16 hours a week for two years, and at least eight hours a week for five years. The legislation doesn't cover small firms with fewer than five employees.

You can get maternity leave for up to 29 weeks after your

baby is born, so long as you don't leave your job any earlier than 11 weeks before your baby is due. Your employer doesn't have to give you back your old job, but you must be offered a similar job and they can't cut your pay. You are under no obligation to go back to work even if you did tell your boss you wanted your job back, so it makes sense to keep your options open. You must give your employer at least three weeks' notice of the date you intend going back to work.

As soon as your baby is born, you can claim **Child Benefit**. Ask for a claim form at your local DHSS office or fill in the coupon at the back of DHSS leaflet FB.8 'Babies and benefits'. Child Benefit is a flat-rate weekly benefit normally paid to the mother.

Most women with children have the right to claim this benefit – it doesn't depend on your National Insurance contribution record. Except where you can demonstrate financial hardship, the money is paid four-weekly in arrears, and you can now arrange for it to be paid directly into a bank, building society or National Savings account. Child Benefit is usually increased each April and the new rate is announced in November. The rate per child in 1987–88 was £7.25 a week.

Child Benefit stops once your children are 16 and leave school. But if they are still at school or college full-time and are not studying beyond 'A' levels or Ordinary National Diploma it can continue up until they reach 19. It stops once your child goes to university. Child Benefit is covered in DHSS leaflet CH.1.

There is an additional payment for single parents – called **One Parent Benefit** – which is the same regardless of the number of children you have. In 1987–88 it was £4.70 a week. Child Benefit and One Parent Benefit are both tax-free. One Parent Benefit is covered in DHSS leaflet CH.11.

Don't forget you are entitled to free prescriptions and dental treatment while you are pregnant and until your child's first birthday. You are normally given the correct form to fill in when you make your first ante-natal visit.

The arrival of one's first child is, for many of us, the most eagerly awaited event of our lives. But that dream of parenthood so often turns into a nightmare of broken nights and lonely days at home with no one to talk to but a grumpy baby. Far from reading all those books we expected to devour while baby sleeps or gurgles in her pram, we find ourselves rushed off our feet with little time to ourselves.

With so much to do, it's not the best moment to think about the future, but think about it we should. Those carefree days when we had no one but ourselves to consider have gone for ever. Now there is someone who depends on us, and not just for love and care but for financial support as well.

It's time to think about what would happen to our family if we died early or fell seriously ill. The rest of this chapter looks at the best ways of making sure your family has enough money to live on if anything happens to you. It also looks at the most painless methods of building up a little nest egg to help launch your children into adult life.

LIFE INSURANCE

On the whole, single people don't need life insurance – it's just a costly waste of money. But as soon as you have a baby there is someone who depends on your pay packet and you need life insurance. Choose the right sort of policy and it won't break the bank.

Life insurance can be very confusing. At its most basic, it offers simple protection. With this type of insurance if you die at any time during a pre-determined period, the insurance company pays your family the value of the policy. If you don't die while the policy is in force, you get nothing.

The confusion arises because life insurance can also be a method of saving. Here, the premiums are more expensive because the insurance company pays you a lump sum when the policy matures.

On the face of it this might seem more attractive than straight life insurance where you often get nothing back. However, the investment returns on life insurance policies are not spectacular. Quite simply there are better ways to save. See Chapters 2 and 9.

It is important to understand the differences between the types of life insurance. If you don't, you are likely to have the wool pulled over your eyes by some commission-hungry life insurance salesman who is pushing savings plans rather than value-for-money protection policies.

But before you rush out to buy life insurance, you need to know how much to buy. If you have followed the advice in Chapter 1, you already know the financial damage your early death would cause your family.

There are two ways of approaching the problem.

- Provide your family with a large lump sum. They can then use the money to pay off your debts – mortgage, personal loans and credit cards – and replace any assets such as a car which went with your job. The rest of the money is then invested to provide an income to make up any shortfall in the family's day-to-day expenses.

- Provide them with a smaller lump sum and a regular monthly income. The lump sum pays off the debts and replaces the assets. The income meets the shortfall in the family's income.

Term insurance is the best and cheapest way of providing your family with a lump sum. With term insurance you decide how much insurance you need (called the sum insured) and how long you need it for (the term). For example, you might decide your family would need a lump sum of £100,000 if you died within the next 20 years.

The younger you are when you take out the policy, the less likely you are to die and thus the cheaper the premium. Equitable Life, whose premiums are normally among the lowest, charge a 30-year-old woman £8.17 a month for term insurance of £100,000 over 20 years. The cost rises to £19.50 a month for a 40-year-old. Remember, with term insurance you get nothing if you don't die within the term of the policy. Term insurance offers protection only; there is no element of savings.

The same is true for **mortgage protection** insurance. You don't need this type of insurance if you have an endowment mortgage. But if you opt for a straight repayment mortgage, your family may not be able to keep up the mortgage payments if you aren't there making your contribution. Mortgage protection insurance is the best way to provide the necessary lump sum. It is even cheaper than term insurance, because the sum insured decreases as your mortgage debt falls. For example, if at age 30 you take out a £30,000 mortgage over 25 years, a mortgage protection policy with Equitable Life costs you just £2.30 a month. If you take out the same mortgage at age 40 but over 20 years, the premiums on the mortgage protection policy are £4.22 a month.

If you prefer to take the second route and provide your family with a smaller lump sum supported by a regular income, take out a **Family income benefit**, alongside some term insurance. Family income benefit pays your family an annual income for a given number of years. So if you take out a policy worth £10,000 a year for the next 20 years and you die after 10 years, your family gets £10,000 for the next 10 years. If you are still alive when the policy comes to an end, you get nothing.

Equitable Life charges a 30-year-old £5.83 a month for an income of £10,000 a year for 20 years. The premium for a 40-year-old is £11.83 a month. You can tailor family income benefit to suit your circumstances. You can choose a plan where the sum insured increases each year, or one where the benefit increases, or both.

Term insurance, a mortgage protection policy and family income benefit are in most cases the only life insurance you will ever need. But you may be offered any one of the following types of life insurance.

○ **Whole life insurance** is a cross between protection and savings insurance. With whole life insurance you normally pay your premiums throughout your life and your family collects the sum insured when you die. You can also ask for a cash surrender before then, but in the early years at least, you get back less than you pay in. The premiums are more expensive than term insurance. Non-profit policies pay out the sum insured, no more no less. With-profit policies pay bonuses which depend on the profits earned by the insurance company. Use whole life insurance if you want to make sure there is money available to pay Inheritance Tax on your estate when you die.

○ **Endowment insurance** is a way of saving dressed up with a bit of life insurance. Tax relief used to be the main reason for investing in these policies. Since tax relief on new policies was abolished in April 1984, endowment insurance has little to offer unless it is of the low-cost variety and linked with a mortgage. See Chapter 5. With endowment insurance you agree to save a certain amount each month for at least 10 years. In the meantime your life is insured usually for not much more than the premiums you are to pay over the term of your policy. If you surrender the policy in the earlier years, you may not get all your money back. With-profit policies earn bonuses.

○ **Unit-linked insurance** plans are similar to endowment insurance. They are basically savings plans with some added life insurance. Depending on the structure of the plan, most of your premium is invested in a unit trust or an insurance company investment fund. You must agree to save for at least 10 years. If you surrender the plan earlier, you may not get all your money back. The best unit-linked policies are better than the best with profit endowment plans. But you do better still investing in a unit trust regular savings plan. See Chapter 2.

SEX DISCRIMINATION AND INSURANCE

Insurance companies are legally entitled to take sex into account when they fix their premium rates, and they do. This is quite simply because women live longer than men. For example, at age 20 a woman can expect to live until age 78, while a man of the same age can only expect to survive to 73[5]. With life insurance, it's a case of swings and roundabouts. With term insurance, family income benefit and mortgage protection policies women are usually treated as being four years younger than men so their premiums work out cheaper.

The opposite is the case with annuities, where you pay the insurance company a lump sum in exchange for a fixed income for life. Female annuity rates are lower than those for men of the same age because the insurance company expects to pay the income over a longer period.

We may wonder why. But there is no doubting the fact that on average women live longer than men. What is curious is that our working lives appear to be dogged with illness. We seem to be sick more often and for longer periods than men. This results in us being charged up to half as much again as men for sickness insurance. It is a problem which has led the Equal Opportunities Commission to ask for the repeal of clause 45 of the Sex Discrimination Act 1975 – the clause which allows insurance companies to take sex differences into account when fixing premium rates.

SICKNESS INSURANCE

Until there is a change in the law, women will have to swallow their pride and accept the fact that they are going to be charged more for sickness insurance. Sickness insurance – or permanent health insurance – deserves to be better known and better supported than it is. Sickness insurance pays you an income if you fall ill and can't work, or have to take a less demanding job and a pay cut. Young people are very much more likely to fall seriously ill than die. And certainly single people with no dependants need this type of insurance above all others. In this instance don't wait until you have a baby before taking out a policy. In fact only 8 per cent of the working population is covered under an individual or group sickness insurance policy, and most of these are self-employed.

Don't count on the State to support you in your ill health. Your employer is responsible for paying you Statutory Sick Pay during the first 28 weeks of any illness. There are two rates of pay depending on how much you earn. In the 1987–88 tax year, the highest rate was £47.20 a week if you earned more than £76.50 a week, and £32.85 a week if you earn between £39 and £76.49 a week. This is the minimum your employer is legally required to pay you; many pay more. But if you don't have enough to live on you must claim supplementary benefit. If you are still ill after 28 weeks you can claim State Sickness Benefit or Invalidity Benefit.

It is not surprising that women find it irksome to pay so much more than men to take out private sickness insurance, especially as the evidence is by no means as clear cut as it is with life expectancy. However, Government health figures do appear to support the view that women are sicker than men. This is even the case if you ignore pregnancy-related illnesses which are not normally covered by sickness insurance policies.

In 1985, dentist Jennifer Pinder was so incensed to find she was being charged 50 per cent more than a male colleague for sickness insurance she decided to sue. With the help of the Equal Opportunities Commission she took her insurance company to court under the Sex Discrimination Act 1975. She argued that women who take out sickness insurance are likely to be highly motivated and unlikely to follow the same pattern of illness as the rest of the female population.

Her insurance company produced figures showing that women claimed more frequently than men and that other insurance companies had similar experiences. Sickness insurance is still in its infancy in this country. The number of women making claims is quite small. Nonetheless the judge accepted that the insurance companies had sufficient evidence to justify the higher premium rate.

But Jennifer Pinder hasn't given up the fight. She says there is evidence that some companies are selling health insurance in a non-discriminatory way. For example, a new short-term sickness policy introduced by the BMA for doctors and dentists charges men and women the same premium. However, it remains the case that most insurance companies continue to charge women between a third and a half more than men for sickness insurance. It is possible to keep down the cost by shopping around. Sickness insurance premiums vary wildly. So much so that the cheapest companies charge women less than the most expensive companies charge men.

It is also cheaper if you choose a policy which doesn't pay an income immediately you fall ill. This is called the deferred period. You can defer payments for a month, three months, six months, even a year. The longer you can afford to wait the cheaper your premium.

If you work for an employer, check your contract of employment. You are almost certainly entitled to Statutory Sick Pay and many employers continue paying their employees for the first three to six months of any illness. Work it so your private sickness insurance starts paying you an income only when your employer stops.

If you work for yourself you start losing money the day you go sick. You are only entitled to State Sickness Benefit. In the 1987–88 tax year this paid just £30.05 a week to women under 60, and £37.85 if you are 60 or over for the first 28 weeks of any illness. This, and your emergency savings, may tide you over the first weeks of any illness. After that you will need your own sickness insurance if you want to maintain your standard of living.

To make sure there is some financial incentive to get back to work, benefit is usually restricted to 75 per cent of what you earn, normally after deducting any State or statutory sickness benefits. There is often a maximum level of benefit. Check this is high enough. Policies can usually be arranged so the benefit increases by an agreed percentage each year. With others, the sum insured and premium can be automatically increased as well.

It seems that no one really wants to encourage women to take out health insurance. If you have an individual policy, rather than being a member of a group policy where you work, the benefit counts as investment income, so if you are a married woman you can't set the Wife's Earned Income Allowance against the income when you work out your tax bill.

The problem doesn't arise with group schemes where the benefit is taxed as earned income. Look at the small print – there are some wide variations in the scope of these policies. Watch the following points in particular:

○ Definition of sickness. Avoid policies which have the right to cut off your benefit if they think you are capable of going back to work but in a lesser capacity.

○ Pregnancy. You can't claim benefit if you are off sick because you are pregnant. If you think you might want to get pregnant choose from among the companies which do pay benefit if you continue to be ill after giving birth. Most of these companies extend the deferred period before meeting any claim. So if your policy has a deferred period of six months you may have to wait a further three months before you see any benefit. But it's better than nothing.

○ Partial disablement. Check if you can claim a partial payment if you take up a job which pays less or if you go back to your own employer but in a lesser capacity.

○ Housewives. A handful of companies (Commercial Union, General Accident, M & G, Norwich Union, Permanent, Phoenix, and Prudential) insure housewives. The maximum rate of benefit varies between £30 and £100 a week, and some policies specify that you must be confined to the house.

MAKING A WILL

Once you have a child you have the beginnings of your very own dynasty. Men are much more preoccupied with preserving the line, producing male heirs, and maintaining the family name than women. So much so that it is not in the least uncommon for husbands but not wives to make a will. Others think wills aren't necessary if you intend leaving everything to your husband or wife. It's a misconception. The truth is it may not matter if you don't have children, but it certainly does once you do.

You may not care what happens to your money and belongings after you die. But would you really like your husband to be forced to sell the family house, or your mother-in-law to inherit the fruits of your labour? It would be bad luck, but it could happen if you died without making a will.

If you make a will there is less room for argument. On the whole only close relatives, common-law spouses and long-term lovers can challenge a will, and usually only if you were supporting them financially while you were alive.

But if you die without making a will the laws of intestacy apply. Under these rules, if you have children your husband gets the first £40,000 of your estate, and a life interest in half the remainder. The rest goes to your children equally. If you are married with no children, your husband gets the first £85,000 of your estate, and as before a life interest in half the remainder. The rest is inherited by your relations.

Where a husband and wife die together, for example in a car crash, the elder of the two is said to have died first. In these circumstances it could happen that your husband inherits the bulk of your estate, and if there are no children both estates would pass to his family. This may not be your intention.

There is nothing to stop you making your own will. You don't have to use a solicitor, although for a simple will they usually don't charge more than £50. But if it is to be valid, you must follow certain rules. You can buy special forms for drawing up wills from legal stationers. Buy or borrow from your library a good book on do-it-yourself wills. The Consumers' Association, publishers of *Which?*, have a book called *Wills and Probate* price £6.95 available from Castlemead, Gascoyne Way, Hertford, SG14 1LH.

INHERITANCE TAX

Almost everyone who will one day own their house free of any mortgage should think about Inheritance Tax when they make their will.

For example, if you died during the 1987–88 tax year and left an estate worth more than £90,000, your estate would be liable to Inheritance Tax. (This threshold is normally increased every year in the budget.)

Thankfully there are plenty of legitimate ways of making sure that most of the fruits of a lifetime's labours are passed on to your nearest and dearest and don't end up swelling the Chancellor's coffers.

Unfortunately it is impossible to predict when you are going to die. But if you get your timing right, in most cases, you can give away up to £90,000 (in the 1987–88 tax year), and if you are still alive in seven years' time there is no Inheritance Tax to pay. And even if you die before then, the final tax bill is reduced on a sliding scale depending on how soon after making the gift you die.

Make use of tax-free gifts. There is no Inheritance Tax to pay on any of these, even if you die the following day:

- Gifts between husband and wife.

- Most gifts to charities, museums, art galleries and political parties.

- Gifts on marriage. Parents can give £5,000, grandparents £2,500, and anyone else £1,000.

- Small gifts of up to £250 to as many people as you like.

- Larger gifts up to a total of £3,000.

- Gifts out of normal expenditure which don't reduce your standard of living, such as payments under a deed of covenant.

SAVING FOR CHILDREN

The building society passbook has replaced the National Savings Ordinary Account as the favourite method of initiating the young in the financial facts of life. And just like the National Savings Ordinary Account it is by no means the most suitable for the task.

The important thing to remember about children is that as soon as they are born they are entitled to their own tax allowance. You only have to pay tax on the income from their investments if:

- The money came from their parents.

- The income is higher than their personal tax allowance.

If grandparents, godparents and friends are in the habit of stuffing five pound notes into your children's hot little hands, put it in a savings account which doesn't deduct interest at source. Your best bet is usually to open a National Savings Investment Account in your child's name. But remember that if your children know about their accounts they can operate them for themselves as soon as they are seven. Before then you can only withdraw the money in cases of extreme financial hardship.

If, as a parent, you want to save money for your children, you normally have to pay the tax on their investment income. There is one exception. If you open a National Savings Investment Account in your own name in trust for your child (ask for Form SB2006C at the Post Office) the income is treated as belonging to the child so long as you make no withdrawals of capital or interest before the child's 18th birthday. The Inland Revenue accepts that the account is entirely for the benefit of your child. A good dodge this one.

COVENANTS

Grandparents who want to give money to their grandchildren on a regular basis can probably save tax if they use a deed of covenant. Money paid under a deed of covenant is free of basic-rate tax, but it is only worth doing if the grandparents pay tax and their grandchildren don't.

This is how it works. If the grandparents want to give their grandchildren £100 a year, they deduct an amount for basic-rate tax (£27) from the payments of £100 and hand their grandchildren £73. The grandchildren then claim back the £27 from the Inland Revenue, using Inland Revenue form R.185P which their grandparents send them every year.

A covenant is a legal agreement to pay someone a certain amount of money each year for seven years. The agreement can finish earlier if both parties agree.

Parents can't transfer money to their children under a deed of covenant until the child marries or reaches 18, whichever is the sooner. So long as your children have unused personal tax allowances, a deed of covenant is the cheapest way of maintaining your children while they are at university or college. You can draw up your own deed of covenant using a special form available from the Inland Revenue. Ask for forms IR.47 and IR.59.

[1] *Social Trends 16* – 1986 Edition, Table 1.11.
[2] *Social Trends 17* – 1987 Edition, Table 2.12.
[3] Women and Employment: A lifetime perspective', The report of the 1980 DE/OPCS Women and Employment Survey, Table 2.6.
[4] As above, Table 4.10.
[5] *Social Trends 17* – 1987 Edition, Table 7.1.

£££

8

Going it alone

Working for yourself is the ultimate freedom. It makes no difference whether you decide simply to take your skills and sell them from home, or whether you have grander ideas for setting up your own business. When you are your own boss, it's up to you to set the pace.

Never again will any boss tell you what to do, how to do it and when to do it. From now on, you are on your own and the only people you need to please are your customers. If this sounds attractive and if you find the yoke of employment difficult to bear, think about working for yourself.

Giving up a well-paid job to go freelance can be an agonising decision. Starting a business on your dining room table after your children have gone to bed may be more a question of necessity. But in the end it doesn't matter what drives you – the important thing is taking that first step. Of course, there is no cast-iron guarantee that you will succeed. But you never know until you try. And if you are really interested in scaling the heights and becoming that woman of substance, working for yourself is likely to be the key to doing it.

But don't be in too much of a rush. Not everyone has the right psychological make-up to go it alone. Ask yourself these basic questions and answer them honestly:

- ○ Am I good at selling myself?
- ○ Am I disciplined and organised enough to work on my own?
- ○ Could I work out a business plan?
- ○ Am I good at motivating other people?
- ○ Have I got good contacts?

- ○ Am I nervous when someone asks me to do something new at work?
- ○ Would I miss the social side of coming to work?
- ○ Would I mind taking a drop in pay?
- ○ Would I worry about my retirement pension?

If your answers are predominantly 'yes' to the first set of questions and 'no' to the second set, you may well have what it takes to say goodbye to the security of the monthly pay cheque.

There are almost as many reasons for working for yourself as there are people doing it. Some women do it as a temporary stop-gap while their children are small, or they are looking after elderly relatives. Some then go on to make such a success of it, they can never face working for someone else ever again.

Others do it because they can't afford to let their skills and contacts decay while they take a career break. This is particularly true of women who work in computers, where you can be unemployable after three years out of the business.

Women with creative skills – designers, architects and writers – are often driven by the desire to do more interesting work, or by the idea of going into partnership with like-minded husbands.

Others break away and start their own business after learning the ropes as an employee. Most public relations companies and employment agencies begin life this way.

Some women are attracted by the idea of franchising. If you have a burning desire to own your own business, but haven't got an original idea of your own, franchising may be the answer for you. With franchising you buy the right to market someone else's good idea. Body Shop, Prontaprint, and Wimpy are all franchise companies.

Setting up a co-operative appeals to women who like the idea of sharing the responsibility of running a business along with the profits. Architects and designers often choose to set up as co-ops rather than partnerships. It can also be a good way to run a book shop or health store, where the cost of employing people is too high, at least in the early years.

And then there are the risk takers. These are the women who see a gap in the market and set out to exploit it with a new product or service. These are the brave pioneers who are challenging the long-held view that women lack the necessary skills to make the grade as entrepreneurs.

THE ADVANTAGES OF WORKING FOR YOURSELF

- You are free to dictate your own terms and conditions of work.

- You can arrange your work to fit family commitments.

- You pay less tax. The self-employed generally pay less tax than those who work for an employer. For example, if you work from home, a proportion of your household expenses are tax-free. See Chapter 4 – The taxman.

- So long as you are reasonably successful, there is no risk of being made redundant.

- You are free to choose where your work is done.

- You are responsible for your own success or failure. Your pay is no longer limited by your employer's pay structure.

THE DISADVANTAGES OF WORKING FOR YOURSELF

- You lose most of the rights you had as an employee. There are no fringe benefits, paid holidays or maternity leave. You can no longer claim unemployment pay, although you are still entitled to State sick pay.

- You must buy your own pension.

- You may have difficulty getting a mortgage until you have three-years' audited accounts.

- There is no career structure.

- You have to do a lot of paper work. Most small businesses find they spend a disproportionate amount of time filling in forms for the taxman.

WORKING FROM HOME

Women who want to combine working with looking after small children can often do this by working from home. For the likes of nurses, doctors, and social workers – in fact anyone whose work depends on direct contact with the public – this is obviously not a practical proposition. But there is no doubt that the combination of the telephone and computer is now making it easier for many people who previously sat in offices to take them home and work from there.

This is particularly true of people who actually work with computers, but nowadays it is by no means only confined to them.

Sue Parker joined F International five years ago as a technical writer working on computer manuals. F International is one of our largest systems houses and provides computing services to some of our major companies. It was started 24 years ago by Mrs Steve Shirley who had the inspiration to harness the computing skills of women who wanted to work from home.

Sue Parker started working in computers when she graduated in 1971. She stopped working for a while when her first son was born 13 years ago, but soon realised that full-time motherhood was not for her. She started working part-time as a freelance.

She says: *'I was offered plenty of jobs, but they were all full-time, and at that stage I didn't want to work such long hours. But I did miss the opportunity of being able to develop a career which you get if you work for a company.'* Five years ago Sue started working from home for F International. She has progressed from being a technical writer to become a key account executive looking after important clients like British Telecom and the Prudential. And now her children are teenagers, she works full-time.

ICL, the computer manufacturer, have run a similar scheme for the last 15 years. They now have 250 programmers, systems designers and technical authors who work from home. The majority are women, some of whom work part-time to fit in with their families.

Many women who start working for F International and ICL from home intend going back to work in an office at some later date. Some find working from home so congenial they never go back. With both schemes there is a career structure, so your work can alter and develop as your family commitments change. Working as a homeworker you are something of a hybrid. You work for yourself in so much as you dictate the hours you work and you are responsible for organising your own schedule. But you are an employee in the sense that your work is provided for you by an employer.

Rank Xerox has taken the idea one step further with its networking experiment. Rank Xerox are encouraging the budding entrepreneurs in their midst. Anyone who works at Rank Xerox and who fancies going it alone can apply to become a Rank Xerox networker. If Rank think the applicant has a chance of making a go of it, the company guarantees them a certain amount of work for the first couple of years.

Rank say the scheme is still experimental. In the four years they have run it, Rank have helped 60 or so people to set up in business. Only eight have been lured back into full-time employment with other firms.

Rosemary Vaux started her own public relations agency in 1984 thanks to the Rank Xerox network scheme. She left Rank with a contract to run their staff magazine and hasn't looked back since.

She says: *'It was six months before I realised it was going to take off. My husband then joined me in the business to look after the bits I'm not very good at: like sending out the bills and talking to the bank manager, and thinking about how we should develop.'*

They now employ two part-timers, a researcher and a personal assistant, as well as keeping four or five freelance writers fairly busy. Rosemary says she now earns more than she could have hoped to earn at Rank Xerox, and she sees plenty of potential for further expansion.

Unless you know you are a born saleswoman don't go in for selling things from your home. Some firms sign up agents, usually women, to sell their goods – cosmetics, kitchenware and jewellery are the most common – from their homes. It's called party plan selling, the idea being that people invited into your home to see a demonstration then feel under an obligation to put in an order. To make money you need a very wide circle of acquaintances, and a larger than life personality. Most people just run out of friends. Not recommended.

Even worse is pyramid selling. These organisations make a blatant appeal to your greed, often in meetings which rely on religious fervour. In fact the only people who ever make money are the people at the top of the pyramid.

The system works a bit like a chain letter. You give a percentage of what you sell to the person who recruited you, and they in turn give a percentage to the person who recruited them. The person at the top of the pyramid gets his cut from every sale. It doesn't much matter what's being sold, although it's often cleaning products.

Pyramid selling is only illegal if there is a fee to join the organisation. Nonetheless, it's a mug's game. Give it a wide berth.

TAKING OUT A FRANCHISE

If you think you have what it takes to succeed in business, but can't think of a good business idea, it's worth thinking about taking out a franchise. With a franchise you buy someone else's business idea and run it as your own business, usually in an exclusive area. There are all sorts of franchise businesses – everything from car rental and hairdressing to hot bread shops and film processing, most of them in the service sector.

Setting up a franchise business isn't necessarily cheap. You pay a franchise fee and then you have your starting up costs. The total varies enormously. It could be as low as £5,000 with a house cleaning franchise or as much as £1 million if you want to open a large Wimpy hamburger bar.

Start your search by writing to the British Franchise Association, Franchise Chambers, 75a Bell Street, Henley-on-Thames, Oxon RG9 2BD. They send out helpful information on how to evaluate a franchise, plus a list of their members. The list is not a guarantee of success, and not all franchise companies are members of the association.

If you like the idea of franchising, it is important to research the idea as if it were your own.

○ Don't take anything the franchise company tells you at face value. After all, they are partly in business to sell franchises.

○ Check out every detail of the package with professional advisers, preferably an accountant and a solicitor.

○ Talk to other people who have taken out a franchise, and not just those suggested by the franchise company.

○ Ask whether any franchises have failed and why?

○ Make sure you are being charged a reasonable amount for any assets or goods you need to buy through the franchise company.

○ Is the procedure for terminating the franchise reasonable?

○ Can you sell the franchise and on what basis?

○ Check whether you are being given an exclusive territory in which to operate.

○ What back-up does the franchise company give you? Do you get help with your accounts? Is there any national or regional advertising or promotion?

Moira Foley took out a franchise with Colour Counsellors, the interior decorators, in 1985. Interior design had always interested her, but with two small children she didn't have the time to go on a two-year training course.

With Colour Counsellors she could organise her work to fit in with her family. She says: *'Many of my clients work and want to see me either in the evenings or over the weekends when my husband can look after the children.'*

Moira Foley paid £2,500 for her franchise with Colour Counsellors. For this she got a two-week intensive training course plus a set of colour co-ordinated boxes of samples. She was now ready to set up in business. But before she took on any clients she had to line up a team of decorators, curtain makers and upholsterers.

Moira's franchise is based in Glasgow and she admits that business was slow to begin with. She says: *'In Scotland, people aren't in the habit of using interior decorators, and in the first couple of years I wouldn't have made enough money to live on if I had been on my own.'*

Now in her third year, Moira is working on half a dozen projects at any one time, and is hoping to get the contract to do some show houses. She says: *'I expect to turn over between £30,000 and £50,000 this year. I pay a back-up fee to Colour Counsellors of £150 a month but if I keep a careful control of costs my profit should be around 30 per cent of turnover.'*

SETTING UP A CO-OPERATIVE

Co-operatives appeal to people who are fed up working in organisations where there are bosses who make decisions, and workers who implement them.

In the ideal co-operative everyone invests the same amount of money, draws the same wage, and is equally involved in making decisions. Co-operatives are not for people who are in a hurry to make money, they are for people who are primarily interested in creating a democratic place to work. Most feminist enterprises are run as co-ops – Sisterwrite, the North London bookshop; Everywoman, the monthly magazine; and Writers and Readers, the publishers, are among the best known.

Not all co-operatives, however, are quite so idealistic. Some do end up employing people, although usually with the intention that they should work towards joining the co-operative. Others, like the John Lewis Partnership, pay lip service to the ideal of co-operation through their annual bonus, but no longer involve everyone in the decision making.

With some notable exceptions, co-operatives work best with a small number of people – the optimum number is probably somewhere between four and eight – who have carefully worked out the aims and objectives of their business.

Co-operatives are normally incorporated under the Industrial and Provident Societies Acts. But they can also incorporate under the Companies Acts, set up as a partnership, or remain unincorporated. If you want to know more about co-operatives the Government-sponsored Co-operative Development Agency (CDA) can give advice, and training. The agency doesn't have money to lend, but it can point you in the right direction. You find the CDA at Broadmead House, 21 Panton Street, London SW1Y 4DR. You may also find there is a local CDA in your area.

Cinestra Pictures is a video training co-operative set up by five women – Rashpal Dhaliwal, Michelle McIntosh, Andrea Stokes, Julie James and Vivianne Howard – in June 1985. The co-operative runs video courses for women covering all aspects of making videos, everything from operating a camera to lighting, editing and writing a story board.

Cinestra are based in Lambeth, South London and most of their funding comes from the local council and the Greater London Arts Association. But they also undertake outside commissions. They have recently completed a campaigning video for War on Want and another on the work of a local community hospital.

Vivianne Howard explains why they decided to set up as a co-operative. She says: '*We didn't want a hierarchy. We wanted a structure that would allow us to make decisions collectively. We divide the work into five areas, and rotate them every six months so everyone gets to do a bit of everything. So far the co-operative only supports us part time. We all work in other jobs for the rest of the time. I like the arrangement, some of the others would like to make Cinestra a full-time job.'*

STARTING YOUR OWN BUSINESS

There are several ways of approaching the problem of starting your own business. If you are starting out in a small way you don't need to incorporate as a company. You can operate as a sole trader and file your accounts each year to the Inland Revenue with your tax return. You don't even need to register your business name. You just have to cross your fingers and hope that it doesn't clash with a name already being used by someone else.

If your plans are more ambitious, or you are going into business with others, you might want to register as a limited company. A simple company registration costs between £125 and £150. Limited companies are legally required to file accounts at Companies House within six months of their year end.

However big or small your intended enterprise, it is important to have a business plan. You need one to show your bank manager when you want to raise money. They are also a useful guide against which to judge your performance.

A well worked-out plan sets out:

- The nature of your business.

- Your intended market and how you have researched the need for the product or service you are selling.

- The nature of the competition.

- Your start-up costs.

- The cost of production, and distribution.

- The cost of marketing and advertising.

- How the business is to be financed.

- How you intend dealing with complaints.

- Cash-flow forecasts for at least the first two years showing budgeted sales, overheads, and profits broken down on a monthly basis.

Anyone setting out in business has a fair amount of red tape to cut through. It is important to make sure you are trading legally before you start. The delays in getting the necessary permits and approvals may cause you months of frustration, but they are certainly less damaging than having your business interrupted once it's up and running.

If you are using a room in your house as an office, you almost certainly won't need planning permission. However, if you want to build a workshop in your garden, or convert your garage into a showroom you must ask for planning permission before you proceed. The planning laws are administered by your local council. Ask them for advice before you do anything. They can tell you if your plans are likely to get the go-ahead.

If you are renting or buying business premises make sure the existing planning use conforms with what you want to do. If it doesn't, don't sign any deal until you have planning permission to use the premises in the way you want.

You may also need a licence to operate. For example, you can't look after children unless you register with the social services department of your local authority. You can't prepare food for sale without regular inspections from the environmental health inspectors. You need a licence from the Department of Employment to run an employment agency.

WORKING FOR YOURSELF AND THE TAXMAN

There are a lot of taxmen after their cut, and like most small businesses just starting out you are likely to go through a stage when you feel you are no longer working for yourself, you are only working for the taxman.

It is important to find a fool-proof and effortless way of keeping your financial records – one which doesn't take up too much of your time. If the feeling of being persecuted doesn't pass, it may be a sign you haven't got a viable business.

You must make sure you have budgeted for your tax bills. There must be enough to pay the Inland Revenue, the VAT office and the Department of Health and Social Security (DHSS).

As soon as you start planning your business write to your tax office. If you were previously an employee, this is likely to be a PAYE office, and they will refer you to a local tax office. Once you know who is dealing with your affairs, it can be helpful to get to know them – they can often be a helpful source of free advice.

Most self-employed people and anyone running their own business are taxed on a preceding year basis. The tax you pay in the current tax year, is based on the profits you earned in the financial year which ended in the previous tax year. Remember that the tax year runs from 6 April one year to 5 April in the next year, and that your accounts don't have to have the same accounting period, you are free to choose your own year end.

For example, in the tax year 1987–88, you pay tax on the accounts which ended in the tax year 1986–87, and if your accounts run from June to June, you are paying tax on the profits you earned between June 1985 and June 1986. You pay the tax in two slices on 1 January and 1 July 1988. There are special rules for working out your tax bill in the first couple of years you run your business, but these generally work to your advantage.

And if you employ people in your business you are responsible for collecting the income tax they owe through PAYE and sending it to the Inland Revenue.

VAT (Value Added Tax) is a sales tax which is collected from everyone in business once sales exceed a certain level. When you first start your business you may not need to register for VAT. You need sales of at least £7,250 a quarter (the quarters end on 31 March, 30 June, 30 September and 31 December) or at least £21,300 a year before you need register.

VAT requires a lot of extra paperwork. It is levied at the standard rate of 15 per cent, although some goods and services are exempt or zero-rated. VAT returns are normally done once a quarter. But from the summer of 1988, any business with sales of less than £250,000 a year has the option of making an annual return and quarterly payments on account.

To work out what you owe the VAT office (or they owe you) take the VAT element in the invoices you sent out during the quarter and deduct the VAT you paid on the goods and services you needed to buy to run your business. The Chancellor hopes to win approval from the EEC to allow any business with sales of less than £250,000 a year to account for VAT only when invoices are paid rather than when they are sent out. This scheme should be up and running at the beginning of October 1987.

There may be times when it is worth registering voluntarily for VAT even if your sales are below the level at which this is required. For example if you invest in machinery or stock when you first start your business, you can only reclaim the VAT you have paid if you are registered.

VAT is administered by Customs and Excise, so if you need further information get in touch with your local VAT office. They also publish a variety of leaflets. Start by asking for leaflet 700/1 'Should I be registered for VAT?', 700/12 'Filling in your VAT return' and 700/21 'Keeping records and accounts'.

You also need to pay National Insurance contributions both for yourself and for anyone you employ. There are four classes of National Insurance contribution, each of which entitles you to a different set of benefits:

- Class I: If you are an employee, you and your employer pay contributions based on a percentage of your pay. Depending on your contribution record, you are then entitled to the full range of National Insurance benefits.

- Class 2: This is the self-employed stamp. You pay a flat-rate weekly contribution (£3.85 in the 1987–88 tax year). You can buy a weekly stamp from the Post Office and stick it on a card. Or, more conveniently, you can pay by direct debit in arrears through your bank or National Girobank account. Class 2 contributions don't entitle you to unemployment pay, or SERPS (State Earnings Related Pension Scheme).

○ Class 3: This is the flat-rate voluntary contribution (£3.75 a week in the 1987–88 tax year) you can make to plug holes in your contribution record. Class 3 contributions entitle you to the basic pension, but don't qualify for unemployment pay, sickness benefit or SERPS.

○ Class 4: If you are self-employed you pay Class 4 contributions on a percentage of your earnings above a certain level. In the 1987–88 tax year Class 4 contributions were levied at 6.3 per cent on the band of taxable earnings between £4,590 and £15,340. Class 4 contributions are collected by the Inland Revenue when they send you your tax assessment. They don't entitle you to any extra benefits.

WHERE TO GO FOR MONEY

Raising money is often the first major hurdle facing any woman wanting to start her own business. Who knows how many good business ideas have failed to get beyond the drawing board for lack of finance?

In the search for money, leave no stone unturned. If you expect to be turned down, you quickly learn the value of persistence.

Find out if you are entitled to:

○ A Government Enterprise Allowance. This allowance gives you £40 a week for the first year you are in business. However, to qualify you must be receiving unemployment pay or supplementary benefit when you apply, and you can't have worked more than eight hours in the previous eight weeks. You must also have £1,000 in your bank account. A letter from your bank manager stating that you have an overdraft facility of £1,000 will do.

○ Grants under various Government schemes. These may be considerable if you are setting up business in a Developing Area, Assisted Area or Enterprise Zone.

○ A loan under the Government's Loan Guarantee Scheme. Your bank may lend you up to £75,000 unsecured if your loan is guaranteed under this scheme. If you can't pay the loan back you are still liable for the debt, but if the bank fails to recover its money it can ask the Government to foot 70 per cent of the bill. The rate of interest on 70 per cent of the outstanding loan is 2½ per cent above the bank's going rate. The scheme is run by the Department of Employment.

You can also get help and advice from:

- A local Enterprise Agency. These are co-ordinated by an organisation called Business in the Community. There are 253 local enterprise agencies, all supported by private enterprise sometimes in conjunction with the local authority. Some have funds available as well. For your nearest enterprise agency, phone Business in the Community: 01-253 3716.

- The Department of Employment's Small Firms Service. There are 13 regional advice centres. To find the nearest to you, dial 100 and ask for Freephone Enterprise.

It is estimated that one in 10 new businesses fail, so it is perhaps not surprising that it is so difficult to raise money.

Once you have exhausted your family, friends and acquaintances as a source of finance, you can try finding a business partner. You can advertise in the business pages of national newspapers or you can approach people running complementary but not competing businesses. Don't expect this approach to be too fruitful, though. Business partners often want control of the business – which defeats the whole object of going it alone.

However hard you fight it, in the end you will probably be forced to approach your bank manager for money. And it is very hard to persuade women that they get a fair hearing when they ask a male bank manager to back them in a new business venture.

Take Anita Roddick, the driving force behind Body Shop, the chain of beauty care shops. Roddick's success has been phenomenal. From small beginnings in Brighton eleven years ago she has built a multi-million pound business with one of the most glamorous stock market ratings. The first time she tried to raise money, her bank manager turned her down – which as refusals go ranks with the man at Decca who turned down the Beatles! She got the thumbs down because she took her baby with her to the interview and that contravenes all the rules.

Some people would say she got what she deserved, and learned a useful lesson in the process. But there is no doubt that women need to turn themselves inside out if they want bank managers to part with their money.

There must be nothing to remind them of the reality of most women's lives – no echoes of snotty children, or piles of dirty washing or forgotten bills. It was only when Anita Roddick went back, neatly dressed, having exchanged her babe in arms for a well worked-out business plan that the bank manager sat up and took notice.

Bank managers don't back ideas, they back bits of paper signed by accountants. They feel more at home with cash-flow projections and profit and loss forecasts than inspiration.

Glenda Hogarth runs Hogarth Safety Wear in Aberdeen. She started out in 1979 when she organised a management 'buy out' of a P & O subsidiary. Her company distributes and makes protective clothing for the off-shore oil industry. She says: *'The figures always looked good so I didn't have any problem raising the money for the "buy out", but at all our meetings with the bank it was clear the bankers felt happier talking to my accountant than to me. Six years later we raised the money to buy our own building and I'm now being taken rather more seriously by the bank.'*

It's an experience echoed by publisher, Jill Norman, who built up Penguin's distinguished list of cookery books before striking out on her own. She says: *'When I first started my own imprint the bank manager would talk to my accountant not me, it was as if I was invisible. Another bank manager took to dropping in uninvited. There was no doubt he was genuinely interested in what I was doing but I also got the feeling I was being watched because I was a woman.'*

According to Jean Watkins, who is now head of the Centre for Enterprise, Research and Learning, few women entrepreneurs have the kind of track record in business which impresses bank managers. Jean Watkins says: *'Women typically set up in business after taking a break to have a family, and they tend to take the plunge at a younger age than men.'*

'Most of the 100 entrepreneurs who took part in my research at the Manchester Business School said women had a tougher time than men raising money. They felt they had to be at least twice as good as the men. However, there was also the view that bank managers were easily impressed by a really professional business plan. Some bank managers seemed so surprised to find such a high level of competence coming from a woman, they leaned over backwards to give the proposal a fair hearing.'

Gillian Harwood is a commercial property developer – a field where very few women have dared to venture. She says: *'I learned the virtue of persistence very early on. Whenever I have asked a bank for money, I do it absolutely by the book. I find partners who are prepared to put up around 40 per cent of the development cost, and I let the bank take my house as security. On two occasions with different banks the same thing has happened. The branch manager has given me the go-ahead only to have his decision overturned by his regional office.'*

Some people might have left it at that. Not Gillian Harwood. *'I immediately fired off personal letters to the chairman of the bank. On one occasion the motor-cycle messenger even managed to deliver the letter personally. I got the decisions reversed almost instantly – in one instance just 20 minutes after the letter was delivered.'*

When Sheila Needham started her printing company, Needham Printers, 13 years ago she didn't even bother to go to her bank as she was so convinced they wouldn't give her the money. Instead she took a business partner, and it took her the next 11 years to shake him off. She explains: *'I managed to whittle his stake down to 50 per cent. I thought I had retained control, but I rather naively gave my partner the chairmanship without realising this gave him the casting vote.*

'I learned a lot about business from him, but there were occasions when he overruled me, which gave me the determination to buy him out. I'm sure if I had been a man, I would have been able to do it my way right from the beginning because I could have raised the money from the bank.'

Marilyn Davidson is a psychologist at UMIST who specialises in women at work. She blames a banking system which has been very slow to promote women into senior management. She explains: *'As things stand at the moment, very few bank managers have ever worked alongside senior women executives. Research in the United States shows that the more men in senior management have contact with women in similar positions, the more likely they are to take women executives and managers seriously.'*

But there may be a glimmer of hope for all our budding female entrepreneurs. Jean Watkins points out that we tend to follow the American experience, but with a time-lag of about five years. In the United States the number of female entrepreneurs is rising fast. We can expect the same to happen here. And the more women who go knocking on the banks' doors, the quicker they will get used to the idea that women are as good as men at running businesses.

As things stand, very little is known about women in business, who they are, what they are doing, and why they take the decision to work for themselves. But we do know from the Department of Employment that the number of women who are self-employed is growing fast – it was up by 42 per cent between 1981 and 1984. Nonetheless men still predominate and only a quarter of the people who work for themselves are women.

There are now two agencies dedicated to helping women develop their entrepreneurial skills, and to find out what they need. Women in Enterprise is based in Wakefield (0924 361789), and the Women's Enterprise Development Agency is attached to Aston University in Birmingham (021-359 0981).

Jane Skinner, one of the joint directors of the Woman's Enterprise Development Agency is convinced that women still meet a lot of resistance when they set out in business. She says: '*Women still don't get taken seriously when they go to Government agencies for advice. They are still asked what their husbands think of the idea.*' And even though much of the funding for the agency comes from one of the big clearing banks, she thinks that women would find it easier to raise money if there were more women bank managers.

£££

9

Putting your feet up

Most employers still put women out to grass five years earlier than men. And yet at 60 most of us still feel in our prime. Suddenly joining the world of the senior citizen with its bus passes and shuffling queues at the Post Office on pension day can come as a terrible shock. For some people stopping work is akin to bereavement – they lose all sense of identity. For others it is blessed relief. Some even go on to achieve ambitions they never had time to develop while they worked.

Whichever way it hits you, retirement is always a curse if you are having to do it on the breadline. And for historical, social and demographic reasons, women are much more likely than men to sit out the twilight of their years in penury.

If you survive to 60, you can expect to live for another 21 years[1]. Even if you want to carry on working you may not be able to. Ill health or your employer may force you into retirement, and with no source of earned income you must rely on your pensions and savings to maintain you in the manner to which you have become accustomed.

It is a cruel fact of economic life that women have at most just 44 working years in which to build up sufficient resources to support themselves during 20 long years of economic inactivity.

Historically, women retire early for the convenience of men.

Men tend to marry women several years younger than themselves. And the idea that they might have to spend several years of their retirement at home on their own without a woman to fetch and carry is obviously too awful to contemplate. So traditionally women retire early.

Even if your contract of employment says you can stay on until 65, your employer has the right to sack you once you are beyond the normal retirement age for similar workers within your company. In these circumstances your employer has sacked you quite lawfully and it's not a case of unfair dismissal. Although following a recent case in the European Court of Justice, from November 1987 it is illegal for women to be made to retire earlier than men.

The idea that women might want pensions of their own has only really been taken seriously in the last 20 years or so. It was always assumed that women would be able to depend on men in their retirement. It was an attitude which even the Government encouraged. Up until 1977 married women could choose to pay reduced National Insurance contributions which disqualified them from claiming the State Basic Retirement Pension in their own right.

Now the National Insurance system recognises the peculiar pattern of women's working lives. Women who give up work to look after their children or elderly relatives can now maintain the continuity of their National Insurance contributions by claiming **Home Responsibilities Protection** (**HRP**).

But workplace pension schemes still discriminate against women, both structurally and in their detail. Only full-time employees who stay with one employer all their working life do really well out of workplace pension schemes. Women rarely stay put for that long and so often get precious little benefit from workplace schemes, even though they may be paying between 5 and 6 per cent of their pay in contributions.

Many other women are excluded altogether because they work part-time. In 1983 just over 11 million people belonged to workplace pension schemes, but only 3,300,000 of these were women[2]. The following year the Equal Opportunities Commission found that 62 per cent of schemes excluded all part-time employees[3]. And of course, most part-time employees just happen to be women.

Most workplace schemes still assume that the woman's contribution to the family budget is somehow not significant and won't be missed. Most women can expect to get a pension from their husband's pension scheme.

The same is not true for men. Figures for 1983 show that in only 17 per cent of pension schemes was there an automatic right to a widower's pension[4]. From 1988, workplace pension schemes will be required to give pensions to widowers as well as widows.

In Chapter One I explained how notoriously difficult it is to put a lump sum value on your pension rights. But it is possible to get a rough idea of how much pension you can expect when you retire. This chapter tells you how. And the younger you start contributing the better.

Saving for your retirement through pension schemes offers valuable tax benefits. But if you think you can do better without those tax benefits, you can save for your retirement in any way you like. For example, if you think property will continue to rise at a rate well above inflation, you might decide to buy yourself a holiday home which you can sell and turn into an income when you retire.

Aim to maintain your standard of living, but remember that once you are retired you are likely to need less money than when you were working. For a start, your mortgage is likely to be paid off. There are no longer any National Insurance or pension contributions to make, and the Inland Revenue gives you an extra tax allowance.

EMPLOYEES AND PENSIONS

If you work for an employer you may be entitled to three pensions.

- The State basic pension.
- The State earnings related scheme (SERPS).
- Pension from your workplace.

THE STATE BASIC RETIREMENT PENSION

The State Basic Retirement Pension depends on your National Insurance contribution record. If you pay full contributions for most of your working life and claim Home Responsibilities Protection for any years you take off, you will qualify for this pension in your own right when you reach 60. See National Insurance leaflets N.P.32 'Your retirement pension'; N.1.208 'National Insurance contribution rates and Statutory Sick Pay rates'; and BI.27 'Looking after someone at home?' (Home Responsibilities Protection).

If your contribution record is full of gaps you can either ask for a reduced pension or opt for a pension on your husband's contributions, whichever gives the larger pension. The State Basic Retirement Pension is a flat-rate weekly amount, which no one would ever describe as generous. In the 1987/88 tax year, the single person's pension was £39.50 a week, the married couple's pension £63.25 a week.

To get the basic pension in full you need to know if you have sufficient qualifying years. A qualifying year is any tax year in which you pay National Insurance contributions on earnings worth at least 52 times the National Insurance lower earnings limit.

In 1987–88 this lower limit – the figure below which you don't have to pay National Insurance contributions – was pitched at £39.00. So in 1987–88 once you paid National Insurance contributions on earnings worth at least 52 times £39.00 or £2,028 it counted as a qualifying year.

The next part of the equation depends on the length of your working life. If your working life is less than 40 years, you are only allowed four non-qualifying years. If your working life is longer you are allowed one extra year of grace. Your working life stretches from the beginning of the tax year in which you were 16 to the beginning of the tax year in which you reach 59 – a period of 44 years. If you claim Home Responsibilities Protection, your working life is reduced by the number of years you got HRP, so long as it does fall below 20 qualifying years.

If you are in any doubt about your contribution record and whether you will get a full pension, you can ask your local DHSS office to obtain a copy of your National Insurance record.

You can delay collecting your pension until you are 65 and earn extra pension. Each year you put off your retirement is worth around $7\frac{1}{2}$ per cent extra on your pension. See National Insurance leaflet NI.92 'Earning extra pension by cancelling your retirement'.

THE STATE EARNINGS RELATED PENSION SCHEME (SERPS)

Not all employees get a pension from SERPS. If your company runs a good workplace pension scheme, it will be 'contracted out'. This is the term given to workplace schemes which are permitted to opt out of SERPS because their benefits equal or better those on offer under SERPS.

But if your company doesn't have a workplace pension scheme or the scheme isn't good enough to be 'contracted out', your National Insurance contributions count towards a pension under SERPS. The benefits under SERPS are not generous. They don't take any account of earnings above the upper limit for National Insurance contributions – £15,340 in 1987–88.

SERPS was introduced in 1978. As a rough guide, if you pay into the scheme for at least 20 years, your pension is worth around a quarter of your salary up to the upper earnings limit. So if you earn £20,000 a year, you can only expect a pension under SERPS of a quarter of £15,340 or £3,835. The actual formula is rather more complicated. See National Insurance leaflet N.P.32.

You are also in SERPS if you leave a workplace pension scheme and take a refund of contributions. When your firm sends you your refund, they deduct something for tax, and something for buying you back into SERPS.

If you paid National Insurance contributions at any time between April 1961 and April 1975 you may also be entitled to a small Graduated Pension, the scheme which preceded SERPS.

WORKPLACE PENSIONS

As we have seen more than 11 million people in 1983 were members of pension schemes at their place of work[2]. These are schemes set up and run by employers for the benefit of their employees. These days most pension schemes are contributory with both employer and employee paying into the scheme. Employees normally pay between 5 and 6 per cent of their salary. There are still some non-contributory schemes where the employer meets the entire cost of providing pensions, but the benefits are usually less generous.

A good workplace pension scheme pays out excellent pensions to loyal employees. But they are totally unsuited to the working patterns of most women, especially those who want to work part-time or take a career break while their children are small. So much so that the average pension of women who retired in 1983 from jobs in private enterprise was just £15 a week, half that of their male colleagues. Women working in the public sector fared a bit better, but still not equally. They retired with average pensions of £35 a week, compared with £44 for men[5]. And as we have seen, part-timers are often excluded from company pension schemes altogether.

So what can you expect in the way of benefits from these schemes? Your pension normally depends on the number of years you are in the scheme. It therefore follows that a man retiring at 65 is better off than a woman doing the same job who retires five years earlier at 60 – the woman having five fewer years in which to build up her pension.

Most workplace pension schemes base your pension on your salary in the couple of years before you retire – called final pay. The figure is worked out by taking a multiple (usually one sixtieth, or one eightieth of your final pay) times the number of years you have been a member of the scheme.

Schemes based on one sixtieth are now the more common. If you were in such a scheme for 30 years, and your final pay was £15,000, you get a pension of 30 sixtieths, or £7,500 a year. Under Inland Revenue rules, a two thirds pension is the most you can take from a workplace scheme.

You are normally allowed to convert part of your pension into a tax-free lump sum. Unless you need the income immediately, take the lump sum and invest it until you need it.

If you don't think you are going to have enough money with which to enjoy your retirement, think about making **additional voluntary contributions** (AVCs). You can invest up to 15 per cent of your salary in your workplace pensions scheme tax-free, so if 5 per cent is your normal contribution, you could invest up to another 10 per cent through AVCs.

AVCs are a good deal if you expect to stay with the same employer all your working life, or you are within, say, five years of retirement. Unfortunately, because women live longer than men, AVCs bought by women often buy a lower level of benefit than those bought by men of the same age. However, from October 1987 you will be free to shop around and buy your own AVCs from an insurance company, rather than having to go through your company pension scheme.

All workplace pension schemes should bear the warning: 'Job changing can seriously damage your wealth.' Until a few years ago, employees often lost most of their pension entitlement when they moved job. Now you have certain rights when you change jobs, but you are still faced with some difficult choices.

If you have been in your scheme for less than five years (two years after 1988) you can either take a refund of your own contributions or leave your pension entitlement with your old employer.

If you have been in your scheme for more than five years (two years after 1988) you can either leave your pension with your own employer or ask for a transfer value. If you take the transfer value you then have to decide what to do with the money. You can transfer it to your new employer's pension scheme if they agree; you can buy a special 'buy-out' bond from an insurance company; or, from the beginning of 1988, you can invest it in the equivalent of a personal pension plan (see page 141).

If you leave your pension with your previous employer, or transfer it to the scheme at your new place of work, your eventual pension cannot be less than you would get if you were in SERPS. This is known as your **Guaranteed Minimum Pension** (GMP).

THE SELF-EMPLOYED AND PENSIONS

If you are self-employed you are only entitled to the State basic pension. But you are also free to take out one or several self-employed pension plans.

THE STATE BASIC RETIREMENT PENSION

The self-employed pay two classes of National Insurance contributions, the flat-rate Class 2, and the earnings-related Class 4. To qualify for the full State Basic Retirement Pension you need the same number of qualifying years as an employee. But a year only becomes qualifying if you pay 52 weekly Class 2 contributions – in other words you can't afford to miss any contributions. See National Insurance leaflet NI.41 'National Insurance guide for the Self-employed'.

SELF-EMPLOYED PENSIONS

Self-employed pension plans are sold by life insurance companies. They are a very tax-efficient way of forcing yourself to save for your retirement. If you are self-employed you can invest up to 17½ per cent of your taxable profits in pension plans. The percentage increases as you near retirement up to a maximum of 26½ per cent.

You get tax relief on your investment and you can back-date your payments for up to seven tax years if you have any unused tax allowances. The money itself is invested in a tax-free insurance fund so, in theory at least, it should perform better than funds which pay tax.

You can also take out one of these plans if you work for an employer who doesn't have a company pension fund.

You can invest your money as a lump sum, or on a regular basis with a monthly savings plan. It is a good idea to spread your investment among a number of different companies, just in case one turns out to be a dud performer.

You could start with a monthly savings plan invested in a with-profits plan where the value of your investment is linked to the profits of the insurance company. With this kind of plan the value of your investment is likely to grow steadily year by year.

Later on you may decide to invest a lump sum in a similar with-profits plan to take advantage of any unused allowances.

You could then think about taking out a more risky unit-linked plan where the value of your investment is directly linked to the unit price of a quoted investment fund. You need stronger nerves – you may have to watch the value of your investment go down from time to time as it follows the fortunes of the stock market. But over the long term, say at least 10 years, unit-linked plans should match or out-perform more conventional with-profits plans.

If interest rates are running high in the few years before you retire, deposit administration plans are a good idea. These work like a bank deposit account but with the added advantage of tax relief all round.

Most plans assume you will want to retire at 60. If you think you may want to retire earlier or later, check whether you have the choice.

Check, too, what happens to your contributions if you die before you start drawing a pension. Some return your contributions, sometimes with interest. With others you get nothing back. If you want them refunded you may have to take out a small amount of life insurance.

As with workplace pensions you can take part of your investment as a tax-free lump sum, the rest as a pension. You don't have to buy your pension from the company which invested it either. You can take the investment value of your plan and shop around for the best pension deal.

PENSIONS AFTER 1988

April 1988 marks the begining of a new era for women's pensions. That's the date when employees get the right to leave their employer's pension scheme and make their own pension arrangements. (If you are in SERPS you can make your own arrangements from January 1988.) Any young women who is uncertain of her future is well advised to lose no time in breaking away. But remember that your employer is not required to top up your contributions – it is a matter of individual negotiation between you and your employer.

With a personal pension plan you become keeper of your own pension fund, and you don't have to rely on the generosity of your employer each time you change jobs, take a career break, or decide to work part-time. But women who have stayed a long time with one employer or who are nearing retirement are better off staying with their employer's scheme and topping up their contributions with AVCs.

WAYS TO INCREASE YOUR RETIREMENT INCOME

As you tot up your various sources of retirement income don't ignore your house. There are several ways of unlocking the asset value of any house you own and turning it into income. The most obvious is buying somewhere smaller and investing the surplus to produce an income.

The other is to take out a home income plan. If you have finished paying your mortgage, you can remortgage it, using the money to buy an income which lasts until you die – called an annuity. The house remains yours and the loan is repaid out of your estate. However, these plans only start to add up once you are around age 70; only then is the income from the annuity appreciably higher than the income needed to pay the interest on the loan. Plans are available from the Halifax and Abbey National Building Societies, and financial services group Allied Dunbar (01-499 0631 or 01-434 3211).

[1] *Social Trends 17* – 1987 Edition Table 7.1.
[2] Occupational Pension Schemes 1983 – Seventh Survey by the Government Actuary – Table 2.1.
[3] EOC Equal Treatment in Occupational Pension Schemes, 1984.
[4] Occupational Pension Schemes 1983 – Seventh Survey by the Government Actuary – Table 10.6.
[5] Occupational Pension Schemes 1983 – Seventh Survey by the Government Actuary – Table 3.3.

£££

PART TWO

£££

10
Know your financial self

Congratulations! You are well on your way to becoming a woman of substance. You have mastered the art of budgeting; you are on first name terms with your bank manager; you own your own home; you have a sizeable nest egg tucked away earning the best rate of interest; and you may have even started your own business. Now you have mastered the basics, the fun can begin.

This is the point at which most personal financial guides leave you in the lurch. This book takes you to places where others fear to tread. From now on the risks are high, but the potential rewards enormous. In Part Two you can find out what it takes to be a successful stock market investor. You can investigate the fascinating and highly technical world of traded options, and financial and commodity futures. You can learn how to plug into women's networks and how to go about this seductive business of attracting money.

But how well-equipped are you for the journey? Do the quiz and discover the secrets of your financial make-up. If you are to be a successful investor you must know your strengths and weaknesses. The art of investment is knowing how to take a risk. Hard work and research are essential, but in the end it's the psychology of the individual investor which makes all the difference.

How do you rate yourself as a financial manager? If money passes through your fingers like water, you are a spendthrift – you have to be forced to save. If you don't enjoy your money and hate spending it, you are a squirrel – you need to learn how to take risks. If you spend much of your time thinking about money you may be a millionaire in the making.

Ask yourself the following 15 questions. What would you do in these circumstances? Don't give it too much thought; you are trying to find out who you are, NOT what you would like to be. Score the answers with the key at the end.

1. Your uncle gives you £10,000. Do you:

a. Buy a new car?
b. Buy a bigger house?
c. Invest in unit trusts?

2. A friend asks you to invest £20,000 in his apparently booming business. Do you:

a. Say no, because it could sour your friendship?
b. Ask an accountant to look at the books before deciding?
c. Give him the money?

3. Your hobby is collecting 20th century first editions. Do you:

a. Actively buy and sell?
b. Find it difficult to part with a book?
c. Never pass a second-hand bookshop without buying something?

4. You inherit some shares from an aunt. The company has just been taken over, and you have made £50,000. Do you:

a. Borrow another £25,000 and buy a yacht?
b. Take a round-the-world trip?
c. Shop around for the highest building society interest rate?

5. You have a good idea for a business. Do you:

a. Decide it's all too much like hard work?

b. Run it in your spare time?
c. Take the plunge and leave your job?

6. You get into trouble with your credit cards. Do you:

a. Persuade your bank manager to give you an overdraft and pay off the cards?
b. Negotiate repayment terms with the credit card companies?
c. Wait until they take them away?

7. You work for yourself and your accountant thinks you should have a pension. Do you:

a. Take out a pension linked to your mortgage and buy a bigger house?
b. Start putting 15 per cent of your income into a pension plan?
c. Tell him you'll think about it when you reach 50?

8. You are travelling first class to Los Angeles and you are sitting next to a glamorous and obviously rich man. Do you:

a. Find out his line of business?
b. Chat him up and get his phone number?
c. Carry on reading your book?

9. A share dealer you once used, and who you know to be reliable, rings you up with a red-hot share tip. Do you:

a. Buy £200 worth of shares?
b. Put the phone down?
c. Ask for the accounts?

10. Some shares you bought have doubled in value. Do you:

a. Hang on to them?
b. Sell them and buy two other shares which you think look undervalued?
c. Sell them and go on a spending spree?

11. Did you think the last person you saw was:

a. Better off than you.
b. Worse off than you.
c. Didn't give it a thought.

12. Your accountant comes up with a complicated scheme for saving you tax. Do you:

a. Jump at it?
b. Say no, because you can't understand it?
c. Say no, it looks like tax evasion?

13. Someone at work suggests setting up an investment club with the aim of doubling your money in two years. Do you:

a. Commit £50 a month and then forget about it?
b. Pour cold water on the idea?
c. Say what a good idea and get involved with running it?

14. Your child's school needs a new science building. Do you:

a. Tap the big corporations for money?
b. Give £50?
c. Organise a sponsored walk?

15. Your employer promised you a rise of £5,000 a year. He now says he can't afford it. Instead he offers you a rise of £2,500, or increased responsibility and a new job title. Do you:

a. Take the money?
b. Take the new job?
c. Resign?

HOW TO SCORE

Give yourself one, two or three points, according to your answer, and add up the total.

1a – 1,	1b – 2,	1c – 3.	9a – 1,	9b – 2,	9c – 3.
2a – 2,	2b – 3,	2c – 1.	10a – 2,	10b – 3,	10c – 1.
3a – 3,	3b – 2,	3c – 1.	11a – 3,	11b – 2,	11c – 1.
4a – 3,	4b – 1,	4c – 2.	12a – 3,	12b – 1,	12c – 2.
5a – 1,	5b – 2,	5c – 3.	13a – 1,	13b – 2,	13c – 3.
6a – 3,	6b – 2,	6c – 1.	14a – 3,	14b – 1,	14c – 2.
7a – 3,	7b – 2,	7c – 1.	15a – 2,	15b – 3,	15c – 1.
8a – 3,	8b – 1,	8c – 2.			

If you score between 15 and 25 points you are a **spendthrift**. You are a bundle of laughs, you are. You have an attractive, happy-go-lucky attitude to life. Money is not your main motivation. But be careful, not every one has your carefree and generous nature. You could end up in Carey Street with no one to bail you out. You think money is only for spending or gambling. You just can't take the stuff seriously. One minute you are drinking champagne, the next it's mugs of instant coffee. If you hit a sticky patch, you tend to ignore the problem and hope it will go away. You always expect something to turn up tomorrow. And sometimes it does, because with your good nature you do have more than your share of good luck. You are the type who never opens bank statements, and letters from the Inland Revenue go straight into the bin. You have plenty of flair and bright ideas, but no will to put them into practice. It's a pity – you may be wasting your talents. Try exchanging some of that jollity for a little application and you might surprise yourself, and have fun making money.

If you have between 26 and 35 points you are a **squirrel**. You have a well-balanced view of money and its place in your life. You are careful in everything you do, and you are unlikely to end up in the poor house. If you have a fault it's your inability to take a risk. You stick to the tried and tested way of building up wealth – buying a house and investing your spare cash in a building society. You don't have much money confidence, and feel ill-equipped to challenge what the experts tell you. Instead you choose not to listen to what they have to say. There is a lot of the squirrel in you. You hoard things. If you do take a risk and buy, say, stamps, pictures or shares, you find it impossible to sell, even if you see a better investment. If you make a bad investment, you find it difficult to cut your losses. You tend to hang on, hoping the investment will come right eventually. You are a worthy person. You work hard both for yourself and others. But you have a tendency to make extra work for yourself and not always very productively. You have a slightly down-trodden view of yourself. You should try and have more fun.

If you have scored between 36 and 45 points you have the **makings of a millionaire**. There is no doubt about it – you have what it takes. You are a millionaire in the making. You have the necessary obsession with money. In fact you hardly ever think of anything else. You have natural talent – your love of wheeling and dealing. You were the kind of child who made a profit out of the school tuck shop, or played the stock market with the proceeds of your paper round. But you also know how to use your talent intelligently. You keep a close watch on the financial scene and you get people working for you, feeding you with new ideas, company accounts and market reports. But you also recognise the value of hard work. Your approach to making money is never half-hearted.

If you hit a problem, you always try and turn it to your advantage. You have a lot of confidence. You know that money attracts money. Buying a yacht is a good investment, but you also meet a lot of rich people who might further your ambition. Your one weak spot is the taxman – you will go to almost any length not to pay him. It could get you into trouble.

11
Joining the big league

The great British Telecom share sale in November 1984 was the turning point. More than two million people bought shares in British Telecom, half of whom were buying shares for the first time. Up until then the City had written off the small investor as, quite literally, a dying breed. Some even said British Telecom was a flash in the pan. But a string of further share sales – TSB, British Gas, even British Airways – each as successful as the last – all confirmed the view that a new generation of investors was now prepared to sample the thrills and spills of investing on the stock market.

Nearly one in five of the adult population owned shares in 1987, some three times the number of five years earlier. Nor is there much evidence that women find the idea of dabbling on the stock market any more awesome than men, and in fact 45 per cent of shareholders are women[1].

New share issues are a good introduction to owning shares. And with most of the big privatisation issues there was never an easier way to make money. In the immortal words of one investor quoted in the *Financial Times* as he queued to hand in his TSB share application: '*I'm in it for the money, like everyone else . . .*'

However, becoming a serious long-term share investor involves rather more than filling in application forms for new share issues.

The first rule of investing on the stock market is to visualise the worst. Most small investors make their debut on the stock market when share prices are surging ahead and the newspapers are full of talk of boom and bonanza. Think about how you would feel if your shares halved in value over a couple of months.

It's hard to imagine when shares are daily breaking new records. But shares can and do fall and it can happen relatively quickly. Shares are properly a long-term investment, and you have to learn to live with their ups and downs. So don't put money you may need in an emergency into shares. And stay away from shares altogether if the idea of seeing them fall in value fills you with anxiety.

But if you are taking advantage of everything the banks, building societies and National Savings have to offer, and you want to make your spare money work harder for you, then you are ready to join the share-owning classes.

If you can cope with the undoubted stress of owning shares, you are likely over the long term, say between seven and 10 years, to do better if you put your money in shares than if you leave it deposited in a bank or building society. For example, £1,000 invested in the shares of FT-Actuaries All-Share index at the beginning of April 1977 would have grown to £5,746 ten years later; more if you had reinvested the dividends. The same amount left in a major building society clocking up interest at the best rate available, grew to just £2,118.

To be honest these figures don't tell the entire story. It doesn't cost a penny to open a building society account. But there are costs associated with buying shares. Your stockbroker or bank sends you a bill for commission, VAT and stamp duty. And there is a spread between the price at which you can buy and sell shares. It can all add up. So much so that your shares may have to rise in value by as much as 20 per cent before you are actually showing a profit.

Commission is charged as a percentage of the value of shares you buy. But most stockbrokers impose a minimum charge (usually between £10 and £25). This puts up the cost of buying small quantities of shares and this high cost of dealing is a very real barrier to investing in shares. So don't consider putting your money in shares unless you have at least £500 to invest, and you are probably better off waiting until you can commit at least £1,000.

GETTING STARTED

Buying shares in new issues is easy. You fill in the application form, send in the money and hope you get lucky when the shares are handed out. No stockbrokers, no commission.

If only it was always that simple. The complications set in as soon as you want to sell your shares. And if you are now convinced you have a future as a share investor, you need to find someone who can buy and sell shares on your behalf. There are three main choices:

- A stockbroker.
- Your bank.
- A share dealer.
- A share shop.

Your best and probably cheapest bet is to find a stockbroker who operates a no-frills dealing service with a low minimum charge. Write to The Stock Exchange, London EC2N 1HP, Tel: 01-588 2355, for a copy of their booklet *An Introduction to The Stock Market*. It costs £1.00 (make cheques payable to The Stock Exchange) and lists the brokers who are willing to take on new private clients. It won't tell you how much commission they charge; for this you need to do your own research. And watch out because commission charges are changing almost daily.

Since Big Bang in October 1986, stockbrokers are free to fix their own commission rates. They can be as little as the 0.825 per cent charged by Discount Brokers International to the 1.65 per cent of the old fixed commission agreement which most firms of stockbrokers still charge.

But the calculation is further complicated by the addition of a minimum charge. So it doesn't always make sense to choose the lowest commission deal. For small investors who are dealing in amounts of less than £1,000 the minimum dealing charge is the figure to watch. For example, if you are buying shares worth £500 you would do better if you put the deal through a firm with a commission rate of 1.65 per cent but a minimum charge of £10, than with a firm like Discount Brokers with its low commission rate but high minimum charge of £25. In both cases the percentage commission comes to less than the minimum charge and you are better off choosing the firm charging £10.

Don't assume you get a better service from a London broker. In fact the reverse may be true. Out-of-town brokers can often offer a better service at a lower price because the cost of running their offices is so much lower. But whoever you choose, don't expect too much. Commission rates are cut throat and unless you are exceptionally lucky you are unlikely to get the benefit of long cosy chats with your stockbroker.

If you opt for a no-frills dealing service that's pretty much what you get. When it comes to deciding which shares to buy and when to sell them, you are on your own.

It's now much easier to buy and sell shares through your bank. The banks have all recently simplified their share-dealing service, although you must still channel your deals through your own bank branch, and the minimum commission charge is generally in the region of £20. In addition, NatWest have 240 branches with a touch screen instant dealing service. Here, you deal directly with NatWest's own in-house market maker, and if you are selling shares you should be able to walk out with a cheque in your hand in under 15 minutes. So far the service has only been available for the big privatisation issues.

Share dealers are licensed by the Department of Trade until the beginning of January 1988, when they will mostly be registered with FIMBRA (the Financial Intermediaries and Brokers Regulatory Association) under the Financial Services Act. Since Big Bang, firms of stockbrokers have been allowed to combine the two functions of fixing share prices and dealing directly with the public. But because there is an obvious conflict of interest, stockbrokers are required to keep the two functions separate. Not so licensed dealers. When you buy shares from a licensed dealer you never quite know which hat he is wearing.

The best advice is to steer clear of licensed dealers and be wary of any offers of no-commission share dealing. In reality there is no such thing. It is a marketing ploy to sign you up as a client. The licensed dealer makes his money by widening the spread between the price at which he buys and sells shares.

Licensed dealers offer a very similar service to a stockbroker or a bank. But they also act as share promoters of second-line, often highly speculative, companies who employ them to sell their shares to the public. Do business once with a licensed dealer and ever after you can expect to be pestered to buy shares in companies they are promoting.

Share shops are places where you can go to buy and sell shares and seek out company information. You can find them in several Debenhams stores, including the big Oxford Street store, and Midland Bank run one in Birmingham. If there's one near you, it's definitely worth investigating.

WHICH SHARES TO BUY?

There are literally thousands of shares listed on the London Stock Exchange. Deciding which shares to buy is a daunting task. You can leave it to chance. And there is a theory that if you choose 20 or so shares at random you are likely to do as well as if you researched your choice. The trouble with this theory is that most people embarking on the road of share ownership can only afford one or two shares to begin with. Using the proverbial pin to choose just two shares is clearly leaving too much to chance.

Before you do anything, sit down and draw up a list of companies for further research. Ask yourself what you know about the industry you work in – which companies are doing well, which companies are getting over a bad patch, which companies have got a promising new management? You may not realise it, but you probably know as much, if not more, about your industry than all those highly-paid stockbrokers' analysts in the City.

Look around you too. Which companies are getting your custom in the high street? Do you find yourself choosing one company's products above the others? This is just the kind of subjective approach which most investment books tell you to avoid. I disagree. Most investment books are written by men for men. But in most families it's the women who do the shopping and it's the women who have the shrewdest idea of who is most efficient at opening women's purses.

Retailers, food makers and fashion companies are often written off as 'women's shares'. Take no notice. After all, there must be a lot of women who saw what Body Shop or Next were up to, liked what they saw and made a lot of money when they backed their judgement by buying the shares.

Body Shop came to the market in April 1984 at around 24p, when adjusted for a couple of subsequent bonus issues. Three years later the shares reached an all time high of 830p.

In August 1982, in the early days of Next, you could pick up the shares (they were known then as Hepworth) for the equivalent of 72p. In May 1987 they were changing hands at around 347p.

But don't just follow your nose, use your brain as well. It's no good thinking you have spotted a company with the right ideas, if those ideas aren't making money. Take the example of Cullens, a chain of up-market convenience stores based in the London and the South East. The shops certainly look attractive, but it was a long time before they started earning profits. In the meantime the shares more than halved in value. In March 1986 Cullens shares stood at around 240p. A year later they languished around 130p.

Once you have a list of companies you think might be worth buying, you are ready to take your research a bit further. Watch out for news of your selected companies, by reading the financial pages of your newspaper.

Buy a notebook and keep a periodic note of movements in their share prices. Write to the companies asking for their last annual report and any subsequent public statements. If the address isn't in your local telephone book, ask your library for a copy of the *Stock Exchange Yearbook*, which lists the registered address of every quoted company. You may even find your central reference library stocks Extel cards. These tell you all you ever need to know about a company, anything from their past history to last year's balance sheet.

CRUNCHING THE NUMBERS

You have probably narrowed your choice down to a couple of shares by now. Even if you have made up your mind which shares to buy, it's worth mastering the bizarre code numbers which the heavyweight newspapers insist on quoting alongside the share prices.

On the next page you can see a selection of share prices as quoted in the *Financial Times*.

But before looking at the figures in detail it's worth getting to grips with the way a company's dividends and profits relate to each other. Take the example of a hypothetical company, let's call it GoodNews plc.

GoodNews plc is owned by its shareholders, and there are 1,000 shares of £1 each. In this case the company is said to have a **paid-up share capital** of £1,000. So if you owned just one share in GoodNews you would effectively own a one thousandth share in the company and you would own one thousandth of the company's assets, profits and dividends.

Last year GoodNews made a profit after tax of £100, and the company decided to hand over half the profits to the shareholders in the form of a dividend.

The first two figures in the *Financial Times* share columns give the highest and lowest share price in the previous year, or in stock market jargon, the **highs** and **lows**. These figures give you an indication as to whether the share you are interested in is rising or falling and how much movement there has been in the last year.

There follows the name of the share, the price and the previous day's price change, if any. The next column shows the **net dividend**; the amount of money the company paid to its shareholders in its last accounting year. Dividends are paid net, after a deduction for basic-rate tax.

Companies pay dividends out of their profits, and there is always the danger that if profits fall the dividend will be reduced or missed altogether. The next figure, the **dividend cover**, tells you how likely the company is to maintain its dividend. The higher the figure the safer the dividend.

SHARE PRICES

1986/87 High	Low	Stock	Price	+ or −	Div Net	C'vr	Y'ld Gr's	P/E
90	15	✠Hughes Food 5p	89	+4	R0.5	2.8	0.8	63.7
224	115	✠Hunter Saphir	223	−1	†2.5	3.2	1.6	27.7
333	247½	Iceland Frozen 10p	332	......	†h3.3	2.7	1.4	29.8
31½	19½	✠Israel (Jack L.) 4p	27½	......	0.5	2.6	2.6	21.3
273	63	Jacob (W.&R.)	266	......	†Q30.38%	2.4	2.6	20.1
£43⅛	£27¾	Kraft Inc. $1.00	£37⅝	+⅞	Q$1.72	—	3.0	—
292	222	Kwik Save 10p	274	−2	6.0	2.9	3.1	15.5
145	83	Lees (John J) 10p	143	......	†2.0	3.5	2.0	18.7
625	510	Low (Wm.) 20p	593	+4	13.5	2.7	3.2	15.5
115	79	✠M6 Cash & Carry	113	−1	L3.55	2.1	4.4	12.6
330	122	Matthews (B)	326	......	†h2.75	4.7	1.2	25.4
170	93	Meat Trade Sup.	160	......	†5.3	1.0	4.7	29.5
249	150	Morris'n(W.) 10p	245	−4	†1.35	8.9	0.8	20.4
260	205	Nichols (Vimto)	245	......	7.0	Φ	4.1	Φ
82½	52	Normans Group 10p	62½	......	†1.9	1.4	4.3	23.0
313	244	Northern Foods	292	......	8.0	2.4	3.9	14.5
97	80	✠Northumbr'n Foods 5p	97	......	R1.7	2.5	2.5	20.5
222	152	Nurdin P'k. 10p	221	−1	†d4.05	3.2	2.6	17.3
245	126	Park Food 10p	200	−5	†4.2	2.9	3.0	16.2
330	157	RHM	314	−1	6.61	2.4	3.0	19.5
*534	370	Rowntree M. 50p	498	+1	†g2.2	2.4	3.5	14.2
492	344	Sainsbury (J.)	476	......	†5.5	3.7	1.6	23.3
174½	121	Salvesen (Christian)	160	+3	†3.25	2.7	2.9	17.5
173	105	✠Sims Catering 5p	129	−4	4.0	2.0	4.4	16.0
		For Somportex see UTS (Recent Issues)						
120	24	Squirrel H'n 12½p	112	......	0.13	—	0.2	—
93	48	✠Sutherland (E.T.)	78	+1	d3.3	0.9	6.0	24.6
790	520	Tate & Lyle £1	754	+20	23.0	2.0	4.3	14.6
96	40	Tavener Rut. 20p	91xd	−2	1.0	Φ	1.5	Φ
489	268	Tesco 5p	487	+7	†5.8	3.6	1.7	23.2
£386½	£155½	Do 9pcCvLn 2002-07	£385½	+11	Q9%	—	f2.3	—
395	220	Unigate	376	......	†9.7	2.5	3.6	15.8
294	217	United Biscuits	273	+9	§9.5	1.8	4.9	14.1
140	82	Do. Warrants (1989)	125	+6½	—	—	—	—
78	44	Do. Warrants (1991)	72	+2	—	—	—	—
183½	138	Watson & Philip 10p	183	......	6.8	1.5	5.2	18.4
£28	£15⅜	Wessanen (Kon) DFl5	£24	+¼	Q9¾%	2.4	1.9	21.8
85	34	✠Wold 5p	45	+2	♦0.75	1.3	2.3	(40.3)

If you divide the profit for the year by the number of shares in issue you discover how much profit is attributable to each share. This is known as the **earnings per share**. At GoodNews, the figure is 10p per share. The **dividend per share** is worked out in the same way. In this case it's 5p, or half the earnings per share.

The dividend cover is the number of times the dividend is covered by earnings per share. In the case of GoodNews, the dividend is covered twice by earnings and is relatively safe.

The **gross yield** is the gross dividend expressed as a percentage of the share price. In this case the gross dividend is used rather than the net dividend which you actually get. It allows you to compare the rate of return with other forms of investment. Dividends are generally lower than the interest you earn when you put your money in building societies, banks and National Savings.

The last figure is the **PE ratio**. Grown men have been known to turn pale at the sight of a PE ratio. In fact it is a simple calculation. It stands for price earnings ratio, and it tells you how many years it would take the company to earn its current share price. It is worked out by dividing the share price by the earnings per share. So if GoodNews' share price stood at 200p the PE ratio is 20 and if it stood at 400p it would be 40.

A high PE ratio can mean one of several things. Either the company is expected to carry on increasing its profits, or there has been a temporary hiccup in the profit record and the company is expected to make a fast recovery. It can also mean the shares are overpriced.

By the same token a low PE ratio often means a company's profits are flat or declining. But it could also mean the shares are cheap. It's for you to figure out once you have gathered up all the information you need to make your decision.

Working through the example of Sainsbury in the *Financial Times* example, we see that on the day in question Sainsbury's share price stood at 476p, unchanged on the previous day. The highest the shares reached in the previous year was 492p, the lowest 344p. The previous year's dividends came to 5.5p, and this was covered a healthy 3.7 times by the company's profits. The dividend yielded a modest 1.6 per cent a share, and the PE ratio reflected hopes of higher profits to come at 23.3.

Compare the figures with those for Tesco, a similar supermarket group, and you find the two shares carry almost identical ratings.

LOOKING AFTER YOUR SHARES

Having made up your mind which shares to buy, you now have to decide what to do with them. If you want to make money out of buying and selling shares, you can't afford to ignore your investment. Your shares may be showing huge profits on paper, but successful investors know that you have never actually made a profit until you sell a share and have the money in your hot little hands.

If you want to become that successful share investor don't think your work is over because you have taken the plunge and bought a couple of shares. In fact it's only just beginning. You need commitment and just a little hard work to keep yourself informed.

You probably chose your shares because the companies are growing fast. This may be so when you buy them. But a company's fortunes can go into reverse surprisingly quickly, and yesterday's stock market darling is so often tomorrow's dog.

The message is be vigilant. Read the specialist investment magazines like *Investors' Chronicle* and *Financial Weekly* for news of your companies, and be constantly on the watch for other companies whose shares may be worth buying. After all, there is no point staying with a share which isn't performing well if you stand a good chance of swapping it for one which is.

Some people seem to have the trading mentality imprinted somewhere in their genetic code. Others have to learn it. If you find it hard to cut your losses and sell a share when it is showing a loss you probably haven't got the temperament to be a really successful investor. Even if it goes against the grain, there must be a part of you that thinks like a barrow boy. It's difficult admitting your judgement was faulty. But until you have sold a share at a loss you haven't been properly blooded as a share investor.

Some investors find it so difficult to cut their losses that they operate a stop loss system. Each time they buy a share they decide how far the share can fall before they take the loss on the chin. Investors who opt for this system usually limit their loss to a fall of between 10 and 20 per cent.

There are several variations on the stop loss theme. Some investors adjust their selling figure as the share price rises. This way they take their profits on a share as soon as the share price dips by a certain percentage. Others set an objective for each share and sell it when it reaches its target.

And don't think you can look at your shares in isolation. The worse mistake you can make as a novice investor is to con yourself into thinking you have the midas touch if the shares you buy go up. They may only be going up because the stock market is booming and you are in the kind of market where you would be very unlucky to choose a share which was actually falling.

You can't afford to ignore the way the market is behaving overall. Check the progress of the various stock market indexes. The most quoted is the FT Ordinary Index, but the FT Actuaries All Share Index and the FT-SE 100 Index (affectionately known as the Footsie) are more broadly based and a better guide to what is really going on.

Remember, when the market goes into one of its periodic nose dives it drags down the good shares with the bad – it is quite indiscriminate. It is also very hard for anyone, amateur or professional, to decide if a decline of, say, 20 per cent in the market is just a hiccup or a sign of worse to come.

However, as an amateur you have a big advantage over the professional. You can sell your shares and run for the cover of the banks and building societies as soon as the going gets rough. It's not the same for pension fund and unit trust managers. They only have limited room to manoeuvre. If they tried to sell all their shareholdings, prices would move against them.

THE UNIT TRUST ALTERNATIVE

If you want to put your money in shares but feel the hard work of choosing individual shares outweighs the fun of feeling involved with the companies, then you are an obvious candidate for unit trusts. With a unit trust you buy units in a fund which is invested in a selection of shares. The price of the units reflects the underlying value of the shares in the fund and can go up and down just like an individual share. Unit trusts are authorised by the Department of Trade, and you can check on their progress in the heavyweight daily papers – *The Independent* is particularly good.

The advice in Chapter Two on choosing a unit trust regular savings plan is no less relevant when you have a lump sum to invest. But one further word of advice: when you invest a lump sum, you must think like a share investor. If your unit trust turns out to be a poor performer, admit your mistake, sell it and buy something which looks more promising. And remember, you can deal directly with the unit trust company, you don't need to use a stockbroker.

BUILDING A PORTFOLIO

When does the fun of investing in a couple of shares with money you can afford to lose turn into the deadly serious business of creating wealth and building a portfolio? It's a difficult question to answer because much depends on your attitude. But you have probably won your stock market spurs once you own six or more shares worth at least £1,000 each.

Now you need to know some of the other techniques investors use to help them keep ahead of the game.

○ **Charts.** This is a purely technical method of choosing shares, based on charting the progress of individual share prices. Chartists claim these charts tell you when to buy and sell a particular share – called the 'buy' and 'sell' signal.

Some people swear by charts; I rate them no higher than reading the future in the tea leaves. But if you want to consult them, ask your stockbroker if there is a chart for the shares you are interested in and what they are indicating.

○ **The high yield method.** This is a way of searching for shares which may be undervalued. Look for companies which offer a higher than average yield, but eliminate any which have failed to keep profits and dividends increasing over the last five years. You may not find many, but if you do you may be on to a bargain, if you can reassure yourself that profits aren't about to take a nose dive. One Oxford college has followed this method for many years with great success.

○ **Recovery stocks.** Watch out for companies which have turned the corner after falling on hard times. Good omens could be a new management team, reorganisation, the launch of a promising new product.

○ **Growth stocks.** These shares never look cheap. They have low yields and high PE ratios. But once the band wagon gets going there can be no stopping a growth stock, especially during a stock market boom. The classic growth stock sustains a high level of profit growth by taking over weaker companies and paying for the deal with shares.

○ **Penny stocks.** These used to change hands for under 10p. Nowadays the definition is anything under 50p or a pound. With penny shares you get a lot of shares for your money, but this doesn't mean you are necessarily getting a bargain. Assessing a penny share is no different from any other share. The attraction of penny shares is that once they start moving upwards they can move very fast. Most penny shares are that way because they have gone through a rough patch. Make sure there is a fair chance they are on the road to recovery before taking the plunge.

ARE GOVERNMENT STOCKS A GOOD BUY?

Government stocks are one of the ways the Government has of raising money from the public and the financial institutions: the pension funds and life insurance companies. Government stocks are traded on the stock market and the price goes up and down with interest rates. They are a good buy when interest rates are high, and a poor buy when interest rates are low. If you get it right and invest while interest rates are high, you get a double benefit: a high interest rate which is fixed until you decide to sell the stock, and a capital gain as the price of the stock moves up as interest rates move down.

There is a wide choice of Government stocks. Once you get the hang of reading the price information in your newspaper you can usually narrow your choice down to a couple of stocks.

The list on pages 166 and 167 is from the *Financial Times*. The first two columns show the 'highs' and 'lows' – the highest and lowest price the stock has reached during the last year. Then comes the abbreviated name of the stock. For example Treas. 3pc 1990, stands for Treasury 3 per cent 1990, which means the stock had an initial yield of 3 per cent when it was issued at £100, and investors are due to be repaid at some time during 1990. Further down, Exch. 12pc '99–02 translates as Exchequer 12 per cent 1999–2002, which tells us that the stock had an initial yield of 12 per cent and is due to be repaid sometime between 1999 and 2002.

You then find the price of the stock followed by the price movement the previous day. The last two columns are the most important. The first gives the running yield, or the amount of interest you get if you buy the stock at the current price. The last figure is slightly different. It shows the redemption yield, or the yearly return you can expect from the stock if you hold it until the Government repays it. This is a complicated calculation which amalgamates the yearly return with the amount of capital gain or loss on the stock itself if you hold it to the bitter end.

Returning to the *Financial Times* you can see that a stock like Treasury 3 per cent 1990 is quoted that day at a price of £88$\frac{7}{8}$, up $\frac{7}{32}$ on the day before. The highest price the stock reached in the previous year was £89$\frac{3}{4}$, the lowest £79$\frac{5}{8}$. If you bought at £88$\frac{7}{8}$, the interest rate is 3.38 per cent for as long as you hold the stock, regardless of what happens to the price of the stock. If you keep the stock until the Government repays it in 1990, you also get the benefit of the rise in the price of the stock from £88$\frac{7}{8}$ to £100, the price at which the Government undertakes to repay it. This raises the overall rate of return to

7.08 per cent a year.

There are two distinct strategies for investing in Government stocks. You can either invest for the short term, backing your judgement on interest rates, in the hope the price of the stock rises. Or you can choose to invest the money until it is due to be repaid and ignore any short-term price fluctuations. This can be useful if you know you are not going to need the money for a while, and want a fixed rate of interest.

There is no Capital Gains Tax to pay when you sell Government stocks. Higher-rate taxpayers can keep their income tax bills down by choosing stocks with a low yearly income. Instead you make your money as the price of the stock rises.

Government stocks with a life of less than five years are known as 'shorts', those with between five and 15 years left to run 'mediums', those with longer to run are not surprisingly known as 'longs'.

There are two other types of stock which don't fit into any of these categories. Undated stocks or 'irredeemables' are stocks where there is no fixed date on which they are to be repaid, such as War Loan 3½ per cent and Consols 2½ per cent. With index-linked stocks the interest payments and the price at which the stock is repaid are adjusted in line with the Retail Price Index.

You can buy Government stocks just like shares, through your bank or stockbroker. But you can also buy most of them through the National Savings Stock Register. Ask for National Savings leaflet 'Buying Gilts on the N.S. Register' and application form GS1 (form GS3 if you are selling) and special envelope GS3M at your local Post Office. For small amounts of stock, say less than £3,000, the National Savings Stock Register offers the cheapest dealing service. But it's a postal service and if you are in a rush to deal the Register can't compete with the speed of stockbrokers.

The biggest advantage of dealing through the register – especially for those who don't pay tax – is that your income is paid gross without any deduction for basic-rate tax. If you buy stock through a stockbroker you get the dividend net, after an amount for basic-rate tax is deducted. Taxpayers must declare the income to the Inland Revenue, but at least you have the use of the money until they send you the bill.

GOVERNMENT STOCKS

BRITISH FUNDS

1986/87 High	Low	Stock	Price £	+ or −	Yield Int.	Red.
		"Shorts" (Lives up to Five Years)				
100 1/32	93 5/8	Funding 6½pc 85-87	99 25/32	......	6.51	7.84
101 1/8	96 13/16	Treas. 10pc 1987	100 5/32	+1/16	9.99	9.40
98 27/32	90 7/8	Treas 3pc 1987	98 21/32	+1/16	3.04	7.35
104 1/2	99 3/8	Treas. 12pc 1987	101 5/8	+1/16	11.81	9.29
99 1/4	92 15/16	Treas 7¾pc 1985-88‡‡	99 1/32	+5/32	7.83	8.96
104	96 3/4	Exch 10½pc '88	101 3/8	+1/32	10.36	9.20
102 5/8	95 1/8	Treas 9¾pc Cv '88	100 11/16	+3/32	9.68	9.12
95 13/32	86 5/8	Transport 3pc '78-88	95 3/8	+1/8	3.15	6.91
102 1/2	93 15/16	Treas. 9½pc '88	100 13/32	+3/32	9.46	9.19
107 9/16	98 5/16	Treas 11½pc 1989	104 1/8	......	11.05	9.12
103 1/2	93 1/8	Treas 9½pc Cnv 1989	100 13/16 xd	+1/8	9.42	9.06
92 21/32	82 9/16	Treas 3pc 1989	92 19/32	+5/32	3.25	9.84
105 7/16	95 5/16	Treas 10½pc 1989	102 3/4	+1/8	10.22	9.10
104 5/16	94 1/8	Exch.10pc 1989	101 13/16	+1/8	9.82	9.11
107 5/16	97	Exch 11pc 1989	104 1/8 xd	+1/8	10.57	9.13
93 3/4	84 1/2	Treas 5pc 1986-89	93 3/4 xd	+5/32	5.34	7.79
110 9/16	94 5/8	Exch 10¼pcCv '89	106 5/32	+21/32	9.63	7.53
114 3/16	103 5/16	Treas 13pc 1990‡‡	109 11/16	+3/16	11.85	9.02
108 1/8	97 1/8	Exch 11pc 1990‡‡	104 3/4	+1/8	10.50	9.09
113 1/8	101 13/16	Exch. 12½pc 1990	108 13/16 xd	+3/16	11.49	9.08
89 3/4	79 5/8	Treas. 3pc 1990	88 7/8	+7/32	3.38	7.08
100 5/16	89 1/8	Treas 8¼pc 1987-90‡‡	98 5/8	+5/16	8.38	8.80
106 1/16	93	Treas. 10pcCv 1990	102 1/2	+1/8	9.76	9.16
86 13/32	76 1/2	Exch 2½pc 1990	86 13/32	+7/32	2.90	6.80
112 3/16	99 7/16	Treas 11¾pc 1991	108 3/8	+9/32	10.84	9.08
94 1/4	83 1/16	Funding 5¾pc '87-91‡‡	92 1/16 xd	+1/4	6.26	8.14
86 1/8	79 3/16	Treas. 3pc 1991	85 5/8	+3/16	3.31	7.13
106 11/32	95 7/32	Treas 10pc Cv '91	106 11/32	+13/32	9.40	8.21
110 5/8	96 3/16	Exch. 11pc 1991	106 13/16	+5/16	10.30	9.14
118 3/4	103 5/8	Treas 12¾pc 1992‡‡	114	+9/32	11.18	9.09
107 5/8	92 5/16	Treas 10pc 1992	103 27/32	+9/32	9.63	9.02
		Five to Fifteen Years				
109 3/4	94 3/16	Treas 10½pc Cv 1992‡‡	105 23/32	+1/4	9.93	9.07
117 1/4	101 9/16	Exch. 12¼pc '92	112 29/32	+7/32	10.85	9.18
123 1/4	106 7/8	Exch 13½pc 1992	118 xd	+7/32	11.44	9.24
108	93 3/16	Treas 10pc 1993‡‡	104 1/32 xd	+9/32	9.61	9.11
120 7/8	103 1/2	Treas 12½pc 1993‡‡	115 15/32	+5/16	10.82	9.19
92	78 1/2	Funding 6pc 1993‡‡	89 5/32	+11/32	6.71	8.13
128 1/8	109 5/16	Treas 13¾pc 1993‡‡	122	+17/32	11.25	9.20
133 1/8	113 9/16	Treas 14½pc 1994‡‡	127 3/32	+21/32	11.38	9.07
127 1/4	108 1/8	Exch 13½pc 1994	122 1/16	+1 3/32	11.07	9.21
105 1/4	97 19/32	Treas. 10pc Ln. 1994	105 1/4	+1 1/4	9.52	9.02
122 1/4	103 1/2	Exch. 12½pc 1994	117 25/32	+1 13/32	10.62	9.16
104	86 7/8	Treas 9pc 1994‡‡	100 19/32	+1 5/16	8.96	8.91
120 1/8	101 1/16	Treas 12pc 1995	115 3/4	+1 3/8	10.38	9.16
79 1/2	68 1/8	Exch 3pc Gas 90-95	79 1/2	+7/8	3.84	6.50
110 1/2	92 1/4	Exch. 10¼pc 1995	106 17/32	+1 7/32	9.64	9.14
126 1/8	106	Treas 12¾pc 1995‡‡	121	+1 3/8	10.55	9.19
133 3/4	111 15/16	Treas. 14pc '96	127 15/16	+1 3/8	10.95	9.31
103 7/8	86 7/16	Treas 9pc 1992-96‡‡	100 15/32	+1 1/4	8.89	8.95
142 3/4	119 1/4	Treas 15¼pc 1996‡‡	136 5/32	+1 13/32	11.20	9.28
130 1/2	108 7/8	Exch 13¼pc 1996‡‡	124 29/32	+1 13/32	10.82	9.18
85 7/32	74 1/8	Redemption 3pc 1986-96	85 3/16 xd	+1/2	3.52	4.97
106 7/8	90 11/16	Conversion 10pc 1996	105 5/16	+1 5/16	9.51	9.18
131 1/8	108 15/16	Treas 13¼pc 1997‡‡	125 3/4	+1 3/8	10.55	9.22
112 3/4	93 1/2	Exch 10½pc 1997	108 19/32	+1 9/32	9.68	9.18
101 5/8	84 1/16	Treas 8¾pc 1997‡‡	98 1/16	+1 11/32	8.94	9.06
41 23/32	40	Tr. 8¾pc 1997 B (40pd)●	41 23/32	+1 13/32	8.91	9.02
143	118 15/16	Exch 15pc 1997	137 1/16	+1 7/16	10.95	9.40
107 7/8	89 1/16	Exch. 9¾pc 1998	103 15/16	+1 5/16	9.40	9.19
88 3/4	72 3/4	Treas 6¾pc 1995-98‡‡	85 3/4	+1 3/16	7.89	8.81

BRITISH FUNDS

1986/87 High	Low	Stock	Price £	+ or –	Yield Int.	Yield Red.
148 7/8	123 9/16	Treas. 15 1/2pc '98‡‡	142 23/32xd	+1 19/32	10.86	9.35
124 1/8	102 11/16	Exch. 12pc 1998	119 11/32	+1 13/32	10.06	9.26
107 1/4	88 3/8	Treas 9 1/2pc 1999‡‡	103 11/32	+1 13/32	9.20	9.04
126 1/2	104 9/16	Exch. 12 1/4pc 1999	121 19/32xd	+1 19/32	10.08	9.24
114	94 1/16	Treas. 10 1/2pc 1999	109 7/8	+1 17/32	9.56	9.14
112	92 7/16	Conversion 10 1/4pc 1999	108 3/16	+1 9/16	9.47	9.13
103 5/8	85 1/4	Conversion 9pc 2000‡‡	100 9/32	+1 5/8	8.98	8.96
133 1/2	110 1/16	Treas. 13pc 2000	128 3/32	+1 23/32	10.14	9.26
111 1/8	91 9/16	Treas 10pc 2001	107 7/32	+1 21/32	9.32	9.05
137 1/4	114 1/8	Treas. 14pc '98-01	131 3/4	+1 1/2	10.63	9.36
109 1/4	89 7/8	Conversion 9 3/4pc 2001	105 1/2	+1 11/16	9.24	9.05
124 5/8	102 13/16	Exch. 12pc '99-02	119 5/8	+1 1/2	10.03	9.23
		Over Fifteen Years				
111 3/4	91 7/8	Conversion 10pc 2002	107 13/16xd	+1 27/32	9.29	9.05
109 7/8	89 7/8	Treas 9 3/4pc 2002	105 7/8	+1 13/16	9.22	9.04
24 13/32	20	Exch. 9pc 2002 (20pd)	24 13/32	+1 7/8	8.96	8.93
139	114 13/16	Treas. 13 3/4pc 2000-03	133 3/4	+1 7/8	10.27	9.27
112 3/8	91 7/8	Treas 10pc 2003	108 1/16	+1 23/32	9.26	9.04
123 1/4	101 3/8	Treas. 11 1/2pc 2001-04	118 19/32xd	+1 3/4	9.70	9.12
112 1/2	91 15/16	Treas, 10pc 2004	108 9/32	+1 23/32	9.24	9.04
60 5/8	48 9/16	Funding 3 1/2pc '99-04	56 7/8	+11/32	6.17	8.24
108	88 1/8	Conversion 9 1/2pc 2004	104 3/32	+1 23/32	9.12	9.02
108 1/4	88 1/4	Conversion 9 1/2pc 2005	104 3/8xd	+1 23/32	9.10	8.99
117 3/8	96 3/16	Exch.10 1/2pc 2005	113 7/32xd	+1 7/8	9.27	9.00
133 3/4	109 15/16	Treas. 12 1/2pc 2003-05	128 7/8	+1 31/32	9.70	9.08
95 1/4	77 1/16	Treas. 8pc 2002-06‡‡	91 5/16xd	+1 9/16	8.73	8.91
107 5/8	90 1/4	Conversion 9 3/4pc 2006	106 17/32	+1 13/16	9.14	9.02
126 3/4	104	Treas. 11 3/4pc 2003-07	122 13/32	+1 7/8	9.59	9.04
96 5/32	80 7/8	Treas 8 1/2pc 2007	96 5/32	+1 11/16	8.84	8.90
143	117 5/8	Treas. 13 1/2pc '04-08	138 3/32xd	+2 1/4	9.78	9.07
31 5/8	24 3/8	Treas.9pc'08 (25pd)	31 5/8	+2 1/8	8.92	8.90
100	76 5/8	Treas 8pc 2009	91 23/32xd	+1 13/16	8.75	8.88
71 7/8	56 5/16	Treas. 5 1/2pc 2008-12‡‡	67	+1	8.19	8.73
93 1/4	74 7/16	Treas. 7 3/4pc 2012-15‡‡	88 15/32	+1 11/32	8.73	8.83
136	110 7/16	Exch. 12pc '13-'17	130 23/32	+2 3/8	9.18	8.14
		Undated				
47	38 3/16	Consols 4pc	44 1/4	+9/16	8.98	—
42	33 7/16	War Loan 3 1/2pc‡‡	39 23/32	+1/2	8.73	—
53	45	Conv. 3 1/2pc '61 Aft.	50 19/32xd	+13/32	6.86	—
35 1/4	28 1/2	Treas. 3pc '66 Aft.	33 5/32xd	+15/32	8.95	—
29 7/8	23 7/16	Consols 2 1/2pc	27 11/16xd	+5/16	9.10	—
29 7/8	23 7/16	Treas. 2 1/2pc	27 11/16xd	+5/16	8.94	—
		Index-Linked				
		(b)			(1)	(2)
120 13/16	115 1/4	Treas. 2pc '88 (297.1)	128 5/8xd	–1/32	—	2.59
113 3/8	99	Do. 2pc '90 (333.9)	113 3/8	+1/8	1.46	2.62
94 13/16	93 1/2	Do. 2pc '92‡‡ (385.8)	94 13/16	+3/16	2.44	3.11
126 25/32	108 1/4	Do. 2pc '96 (267.9)	126 25/32	+17/32	3.09	3.48
109 25/32	94 1/2	Do 2 1/2pc '01 (308.8)	109 25/32xd	+13/32	3.30	3.57
108 13/32	93 5/8	Do. 2 1/2pc '03 (310.7)	108 13/32	+5/16	3.28	3.53
111 19/32	96 1/2	Do. 2pc '06 (274.1)	111 19/32	+5/16	3.27	3.47
106 15/32	92	Do. 2 1/2pc '09 (310.7)	106 15/32	+3/8	3.23	3.42
111 27/32	96 3/4	Do. 2 1/2pc '11 (294.1)	111 27/32	+3/16	3.21	3.39
93 7/8	80 11/16	Do. 2 1/2pc '13 (351.9)	93 7/16	+1/16	3.16	3.35
101 3/4	87 9/16	Do. 2 1/2pc '16 (322.0)	101 13/32	–1/16	3.15	3.31
100	85 3/4	Do. 2 1/2pc '20 (327.3)	99 1/2xd	+1/16	3.11	3.27
84 13/16	77 3/4	Do. 2 1/2pc '24 ‡‡(385.3)	84 3/8	–1/32	3.08	3.22

Prospective real redemption rate on projected inflation of (1) 10% and (2) 5%. (b) Figures in parentheses show RPI base month for indexing, ie 8 months prior to issue. RPI for June 1986: 385.8 and for January 1987: 394.5.

DECIPHERING THE JARGON

Small enclosed worlds always develop their own jargon, their own shorthand. The stock market is no exception. It can be very discouraging and a very effective way of intimidating the novice. Don't let them blind you with their secret language. Use this glossary to crack the code.

○ **The account** is the Stock Exchange accounting period which usually lasts two weeks. Once you are accepted as creditworthy by a stockbroker, you can deal on account, and you don't have to pay for your shares until 10 days after the account is over. Dealing in the account is the dangerous practice of buying more shares than you can afford, and selling them within the same account period, hopefully at a profit which more than covers your dealing costs. Not recommended.

○ **A bargain** has nothing to do with value-for-money. It is quite simply the transaction to buy or sell some shares.

○ **A bear market** is the term used to describe a falling stock market. If someone says they are **bearish**, they think the market is going down.

○ **Blue chips** are shares in large well-run companies considered to be ultra-safe investments. Companies like BP, ICI, Marks & Spencer and Unilever qualify as blue chip shares. Nowadays also known as alpha stocks.

○ **A bull market** is the opposite of a bear market. The term used to describe a rising stock market. If someone says they are **bullish**, they are telling you they think the market is going up.

○ **The Business Expansion Scheme** is a highly speculative investment only worth investigating if you pay a lot of income tax. Companies which can't raise money any other way can apply to the Inland Revenue for approval under the Business Expansion Scheme. If approved, investors get full tax relief on any money they invest in the company so long as they keep it there for at least five years. If you pay tax at 60 per cent, and invest £1,000 in such a company it effectively only costs you £400. Many of these companies have gone bust, but you can spread your risk by investing in a fund which holds more than one investment. The Inland Revenue issues a leaflet IR.51 'The Business Expansion Scheme'.

○ **Dividends** are the payments of income made, usually twice a year, by companies to their shareholders. If you buy a share which is referred to as **ex-dividend** you don't have the right to the last dividend payment. On the other hand if you buy them as **cum-dividend**, you do get the dividend.

○ **Equities** is just another name for company shares.

○ **A flotation** is when a company sells its shares to the public for the first time, usually with a new issue. The shares are then traded on the Stock Exchange.

○ **Over-the-counter** shares (OTC for short) are shares in often small, speculative companies usually promoted by licensed dealers who make a market in the shares. It can be difficult to sell shares in OTC companies so beware.

○ **Par** or nominal value is the original price of a share or fixed interest investment. With most shares it's 25p; Government stocks are £100.

○ **Partly-paid** shares are those on which a second or third instalment is still owing. The shares in many of the big new issues – British Telecom, TSB and British Gas – have been sold as partly-paid shares, with second and sometimes third payments due later.

○ **Perks.** Some companies offer perks, usually a discount, to their shareholders. There are over 100 companies offering perks – anything from Sketchley's 25 per cent discount on dry cleaning to Barratt's £1,000 off the price of a new £50,000 home. Lists of shareholder perks are available from stockbrokers Kleinwort

Grieveson, 20 Fenchurch Street, London EC3P 3DB, 01-623 8000, and Seymour Pierce & Co, at 10 Old Jewry, London EC2R 8EA, Tel. 01-628 4981.

○ **Plc** stands for public limited company.

○ **A rights issue** is when a company asks its shareholders to buy new shares in the company. The shares are usually sold at a discount to the existing shares. If you don't want to buy the shares, you can sell your 'rights' in the market or decline the new shares.

○ **A scrip issue** or bonus issue is a free issue of shares. It's a technical exercise and in theory the value of your total holding should remain the same. However a scrip issue often acts as a psychological boost to the shares and you can usually count on it increasing the value of your holding. A one-for-one scrip issue is where you get one new share for each one you already hold. A one-for-two scrip is where you get one share for every two you already hold, and so on.

○ **SIB** is short for Securities and Investments Board, the new regulatory body set up under the Financial Services Act 1986 to protect investors. You can find SIB at 3 Royal Exchange Buildings, London EC3V 3NL, Tel. 01-283 2474.

○ **Unlisted Securities Market** – usually referred to as the USM – is a share market run by the Stock Exchange for companies which aren't yet large enough to go for a full quote on the Stock Exchange. The shares are generally more speculative than those with full listings.

[1] Treasury
[2] *Social Trend* 17, 1987, Chart 5.21.

£££

12
Passionate about Coalport

Don't expect your building society passbook to cut much of a dash on your mantelpiece. Nor is there a lot you can do with a pile of share certificates except file them.

There are a lot of people who wouldn't be seen dead investing in stock and shares. Instead they make their fortunes rather more discreetly out of buying and selling the things they collect. If you are the kind of person who likes to deny the capitalist instinct inherent in gambling on the stock market, think about becoming a collector instead.

No painting, piece of furniture, or porcelain figure ever paid an annual dividend. But at least you have a beautiful object to admire and treasure while you watch its value appreciate. You may even have the last laugh on your more aggressive share investor friends. If you are lucky, or choose wisely, history shows that over the long term you are likely to make more money putting your savings into things rather than into shares.

The key to becoming a successful collector is finding a passionate interest. Without some knowledge of what you are doing, you can easily fall prey to unscrupulous dealers who can spot the novice a mile off.

Some people have a flair for spotting tomorrow's rage. They pick up odds bits and pieces at flea market prices which go on to form the basis of valuable collections.

Television personality Janet Street-Porter is a case in point. She started collecting art deco twenty years ago, long before anyone was remotely interested. She has recently sold the bulk of her collection to finance the restoration of a fine 18th-century house in the Spitalfields area of East London.

Most people don't possess that kind of sixth sense. Buying junk at flea markets is fun, but unless you are absolutely sure you are on to a winner, don't con yourself into thinking that a pretty dish which cost you £15 is just waiting to turn itself into a priceless antique. The chances are it isn't.

If you are collecting with the dual aim of having nice things around you which will also appreciate in value, then you must think big. Surprisingly, there are few serious women collectors, which probably says more about our lack of money than our lack of ability. Successful collectors need visual flair and they must be able to pay attention to detail; all qualities which women possess in abundance. What we haven't had until recently is enough money of our own to launch ourselves as serious collectors, which must be why most of the big collectors are still men.

There is also the question of opportunity. Even the busiest man can find an hour at lunchtime to visit a city centre saleroom, whereas most women, stuck in the suburbs perhaps, juggling small children and a job, quite literally haven't the time.

It's also a comment on how few chances there are for women to make money, that so many successful women collectors end up dealing in antiques for a living.

GETTING STARTED

The public library is the best place to embark upon your career as a collector. Knowledge is the first thing you need to acquire. Most libraries have a good selection of art books and antique guides. They are popular, so it could be several visits before you find anything which really interests you.

Once you know what you are going to collect, buy the books on the subject, visit any museums and historic houses with collections, and seek out the specialist dealers.

Collecting is a long-term investment. Don't expect to double your money overnight. In fact it is absolutely essential that you don't put your money into antiques if you may need it soon. Most dealers mark up the goods they sell by at least 100 per cent, so you are unlikely to get anything like your money back if you try and sell too soon.

Beginners are better off sticking to auctions. If the price goes too high you can always stop bidding. And if you are successful, the auction house charges you 10 per cent – the buyer's premium – for its service. Unfortunately auctions are rarely held at times which are convenient for working people. But you can get round the problem by leaving your bid with the auctioneer.

WHEN IS A COLLECTOR A DEALER?

It is estimated that dealers buying and selling to each other account for at least 90 per cent of all deals done in the antique trade. Anyone who becomes an expert in a narrow field, and who keeps a close watch on the way the market is moving, finds that the line between dealing and collecting becomes blurred.

You may even find yourself tempted to do a bit of trading yourself. If you really know your subject you can spot a bargain and you know the other collectors in your field and their little foibles. Matching the two up and making a profit is a time-honoured byproduct of the knowledge you have acquired. Some of the most successful collectors finance their hobby this way.

Collecting isn't a cheap hobby. Enthusiastic collectors clock up thousands of miles each year in search of a bargain. And while stocks and shares pay you a dividend every year, collections actually cost you money to run. The most obvious expense is insurance. Make sure you are properly insured. If you are in any doubt about the cover in your home contents policy, consult the insurance company. You may need to give them a separate list of all items over a certain amount. The banks charge for keeping things like jewellery and coins in a safe deposit box. And if you buy wine you may need to pay a wine merchant to store it for you.

IS IT WORTH IT?

So how easy is it to make money as a collector? Alternative investment expert Robin Duthy keeps a close watch on what happens in the world's auction rooms. He estimates that since 1975 £1,000 invested in any of the following: American coins, vintage claret, American Impressionist paintings, vintage port, 18th-century English portrait paintings, vintage champagne and Georgian furniture, produced better results than if it had been invested in the shares of the FT 30 share index with the dividend income reinvested.

For example £1,000 invested in American coins in 1975 increased at least tenfold to £10,616, compared with £5,509 for the FT 30-share index.

Which is not to say that some collectors didn't get their fingers burned. Diamonds, Greek and Roman coins, English coins, gold, British stamps and the Barbizon school of painting have all failed to keep up with inflation since 1975.

Diamonds collect the wooden spoon. They managed to rise by just 22 per cent, well below the 129 per cent rise in the cost of living.

Collectors also get a better tax deal than share investors when they sell. Most collectors' items, whether they are paintings, furniture or ceramics, are liable to Capital Gains Tax when you sell them. You are allowed to make capital gains of up to a certain amount each year without having to pay tax. (The figure was £6,600 in the 1987–88 tax year.) But if you sell a collector's item for less than £3,000 the gain is tax-free and doesn't count towards the tax-free allowance. You could, for example, sell 10 items, but so long as each was sold for less than £3,000 there would be no Capital Gains Tax to pay.

There are even special rules when you sell something for more than £3,000. Here the gain is taken to be the lower of the actual gain or the selling price less £3,000 times $\frac{5}{3}$. For example, if you buy something for £1,000 and then sell it for £4,000 you have made a capital gain of £3,000. But if you apply the special rule, the capital gain comes to just £1,667. To work it out you deduct £3,000 from your selling price (£4,000). In this case it produces a figure of £1,000 and $\frac{5}{3}$ of that is £1,667.

And if you collect British money, and that includes gold coins minted after 1837, there is no Capital Gains Tax to pay at all.

THE COLLECTORS

Sarah Baddiel has one of the world's finest collections of golfing memorabilia. It all started ten years ago. She was a second-hand book dealer and someone asked her to look out for golfing books. In her search she came across a little Art Deco figure of a lady golfer. She bought it, and when she got it home her family were so enchanted that they pleaded with her to keep it. She was hooked.

She collects almost anything to do with golf: pictures, books, china, ceramics, silver and jewellery, although she draws the line at golfing equipment. For Sarah Baddiel collecting is an obsession. She travels twice or three times a year to the United States where she is a leading member of the Golf Collectors' Society.

And what started out as a harmless little sideline has turned into a flourishing business. As far as she knows there are only two shops specialising in golfing memorabilia anywhere in the world; one in the United States, in Cincinnati, and her own in Grays Antique Market in London's West End.

Including all the ephemera such as old menus for the likes of the Neasden Golf Club, postcards and cigarette cards, Sarah reckons there must be between 2,500 and 3,000 separate items in her collection. There are over 600 books alone. It must be worth a fortune. But like all true collectors, she refuses to put a value on it.

Sarah explains what motivates her: '*I only deal because it's the best way I know of enhancing my own collection. I collect because the subject fascinates me, and there is hardly a day when I don't learn something new.*'

As for her favourite items. She says they are not the most valuable, but she would never part with a tiny turn-of-the-century photograph, just an inch square, of a lady golfer mounted in a miniature frame decorated with cross clubs, or an exquisitely painted plate commemorating the Gibson girl, a famous American golfer.

Roberta Etter is an American with a passion for old photographs and photographic equipment. You could say she was almost born to it: her father is a photographer, her mother a museum curator. It all started when her father asked her to look out for a particular sort of early camera with a round negative. Roberta explains: '*I bought the wrong camera several times, and when I finally found the right one my father was no longer interested in it. But it didn't matter because by that time I was hooked on collecting.*'

Roberta started out with the intention of becoming a photographer like her father. She even had her own studio in Oklahoma. But it wasn't long before the truth dawned on her that she was spending more time collecting than she was taking photographs, and it was collecting which was giving her the most pleasure.

Just like Sarah Baddiel, Roberta started dealing in order to improve her own collection, and the dealing turned into a business.

Roberta says the excitement of dealing comes from spotting bargains because you know a little bit more than the dealer you are buying from. It has also been her passport to the world. She explains: '*Before I came to live in London, I used to visit regularly. I'd buy one or two things here which I knew collectors in the States were looking for, and that would pay for my trip.*'

Roberta's most exciting find, although not her most valuable, was an 1880 Lilliput detective camera, a tiny camera concealed in a ladies' handbag, the kind you almost expect to see in a Humphrey Bogart film.

She says: '*It was in my early days as a collector, when I used to advertise quite a bit. I received a letter from someone telling me they had one of these cameras and would I like to see it. I drove through the night, not expecting it to be genuine. I arrived early and slept in the car outside the man's house. When I finally got to see the camera, there was no doubt that it was the real thing. The owner wasn't sure if he wanted to sell it, but he clearly didn't know how valuable it was. In the end I told him how much it was worth. We ended up good friends, I sold some other photographic equipment for him, and he gave me the camera.*'

The most expensive, but not favourite, item in her collection is an early camera, a Daguerreotype camera dating from the 1840s, worth around £5,000. Her favourite item, because she loves the sea, is a Daguerreotype of a sailor.

Roberta obviously knows how cameras work. But she says this isn't absolutely essential when you collect cameras and photographs. '*It's more important to know the history and have a good aesthetic eye for what looks right so you can spot whether things have been tampered with or fixed.*'

It was their investment potential which originally attracted Mary Butcher to Baxter prints. George Baxter was a popular Victorian artist who invented his own method of colour printing. His prints depict typical scenes of Victorian life – children, families, everyday life and national events.

Mary Butcher remembers how it was a series of coincidences which got her started. '*It was 1970. I saw an article on Baxter prints in the* Financial Times *and what a good investment they were. Not long after that I was chatting to one of the mothers outside my daughter's school. She was an antique dealer and she mentioned she had just acquired a small collection of Baxter prints. I forgot all about it until I saw another enthusiastic newspaper article, this time in* The Guardian. *By then I knew there were a lot of fakes around. I asked the antique collector if she could guarantee the authenticity of her collection. She said she could, and I took the plunge and bought them.*

'*I still have some of those prints on my wall today. They are a reminder of my early mistakes. They turned out to be fakes!*'

While her children were still young Mary Butcher collected locally and by post and her collection grew slowly. She started going to sales at Phillips, the auctioneers, in 1973, and by 1980 she had acquired 150 prints.

It was at this point that a gentle hobby became an obsession. Mary Butcher explains: '*I spent a lot of money on a large collection. Since then I've not missed a single sale at Phillips, and I now have between 600 and 700 Baxter prints.*'

In fact Baxter only did around 400 prints, but as Mary Butcher points out there are endless variations in the details: there may be three or four different mounts and changes of tint. '*I find the study of these prints completely absorbing. The prints themselves are beautiful, and at the same time I've had to learn the techniques of production: the engraving, the printing and the types of paper he used.*'

Mary Butcher has never been tempted to turn her obsession into a business, and she actually finds it very difficult to part with anything from her collection, which is now worth a lot of money.

When she started, good quality Baxter prints changed hands for between £10 and £20. Now you can pay between £60 and £80, and very rare examples like the early Butterfly print can fetch up to £400 at auction.

Interestingly, a look at the history of Baxter prints provides a useful insight into the fickleness of public taste. Baxter prints were all the rage in the 1920s. In 1924 a pair of rare Baxter prints were sold for £900, prices which have never been seen again. That same year a Constable sold at auction for just £39, a Gainsborough for £68.

£££

13
For the woman who has everything

If you think you have won your spurs as a stock market investor, and your nerves are truly made of steel, you might like to find out if you have the makings of a speculator.

The place to start is the traded options market, where for a relatively small outlay you can have some fun betting on the share movements of a number of leading shares. But remember, traded options are as close as you can get to gambling, short of staking your shirt on the 2.30 at Haydock Park. With traded options you can make a lot of money very quickly, but you can equally well lose it all. So never stake any money you think your might regret losing.

The big speculators spend their days glued to their electronic screens watching and waiting for that one price to move out of line before they pounce. Unless you work in the City and have access to this kind of information, you will have to rely on your own research and any help you can find from a broker.

But avoid like the plague any broker who rings you up out of the blue offering to invest your money in such a high-risk investment. A lot of people have lost a lot of money that way. Find your own broker instead. Many of the big stockbroking firms, such as Phillips and Drew, now have departments which specialise in traded options. Some dealers are absolute enthusiasts, so much so you may find you get a lot more advice and help when you invest in something like traded options than when you invest in shares.

Traded options give you the right to buy or sell a certain share at some time in the future at a price which is fixed today. That's the theory. In practice you aren't interested in buying or selling the underlying shares – with traded options all you do is trade bits of paper in the hope of making a fast buck.

To take the very simplest example: shares in GoodNews plc are standing at 200p in the market. For 20p you can acquire an option to buy shares in GoodNews at 200p at any time during the next month. As luck would have it, the day after you acquire your option, shares in GoodNews rise 10p to 210p. The option also rises by 10p from 20p to 30p, a rise of 50 per cent, and you decide to sell your option. On the other hand, the price of GoodNews could have moved against you, or only moved slowly, in which case the whole of your investment could have easily been wiped out.

In spite of all the risks, options do have one big advantage over a direct investment in shares – you can actually make money when prices are falling.

There are two technical terms which are always associated with traded options. They are used as a kind of shorthand between dealers, and are designed to befuddle the novice.

○ **A call option** is the right to buy your chosen investment sometime in the future but at today's prices. You take out a call when you expect the price to rise.

○ **A put option** is the right to sell your chosen investment sometime in the future at today's price. You take out a put when you expect the price to fall.

The Stock Exchange opened its traded options market in April 1978 following the success of traded options on the Chicago Board Option Exchange. For the private investor traded options are normally a high-risk investment. But there is another side to traded options. Professional fund managers – the big investors who look after the pension funds, unit trusts and life funds – use traded options as a kind of insurance policy, usually to protect profits on their portfolios against a downturn in the market.

By April 1987 the Stock Exchange had introduced 49 traded options on company shares, two on Government stocks, two currency options, and one on the FT-SE 100 Index.

FUTURES TRADING

You can bet on the future price of almost anything. In London there are markets for trading the future price of, among other things, coffee, cocoa, aluminium, interest rates, exchange rates, even the FT-SE 100 Index. But unless you become a real enthusiast, futures trading is best left to the market professionals, because the contracts and the sums of money involved effectively rule out the amateur. Futures contracts follow the same general principle as traded options – you acquire the right to buy or sell something at sometime in the future.

Futures contracts are essentially easier to understand than options. The futures price always bears a close resemblance to the underlying investment. Think of a sack of potatoes. Today's price of a sack of potatoes is £5. But for 50p (your deposit or margin) you can acquire a futures contract which gives you the right to buy (a call) or sell (a put) that sack of potatoes in three months' time at £6 (the futures price). You think the price will rise, so you take out a call. You are right and the price of the futures contract rises to £7. You can sell your futures contract and make a profit of £1 (the difference between £7 and £6), all for an initial investment (margin) of just 50p.

Of course things don't always work out as you plan. If the price of the future falls to £5, you lose a pound, which is double your initial margin, and you must make up the loss. It is important to realise that unlike traded options, with futures your risk is greater than your initial investment.

All markets need speculators if they are to work efficiently. They are the lubrication which keeps any market turning. Without them there wouldn't be enough buyers and sellers to give the big institutional users the ready market they need when they want to make quick decisions. But in the case of futures, the successful speculators operate at the highest levels of sophistication. If you are tempted to learn more about financial futures, write to the London International Financial Futures Exchange, Royal Exchange, London EC3V 3PJ.

There are three principal London-based commodity futures exchanges. The London Metal Exchange, c/o Brian Reidy & Associates, Plantation House, Fenchurch Street, London EC3M 3AP, deals in metals: copper, lead, zinc, nickel, aluminium, and silver; the London Commodity Exchange and the Agricultural Futures Exchange deal in what are known as the 'softs'. The London Commodity Exchange, 1 Commodity Quay, St Katharine Dock, London E1 NAX, deals in cocoa, coffee and sugar; the Agricultural Exchange, Baltic Exchange Chambers, 24 St Mary Axe, London EC3P 8EP, deals in wheat, barley, potatoes, meat and soyabean meal. You can write to any of these exchanges for further information.

BETTING ON THE INDEX

Fancy a flutter on the stock market without all the bother of choosing the right share? Why not try betting. You can place bets on two of the main stock market indexes – the FT 30-share Index and the FT-SE 100 Index (the Footsie). There are two specialist bookmakers who will take your bets. Choose from City Index, Europe House, World Trade Centre, London E1 9AA, tel: 01-283 3667 and IG Index, 9–11 Grosvenor Gardens, London SW1W 0BD, tel: 01-828 7233.

Here's how it works. Say the FT Index stands at 1500, the bookies will quote you a price of, say, 1498 if you want to sell the index, and 1552 if you want to buy it. With City Index you can bet as little as a pound for each point of movement in the index. With IG Index the minimum investment is £5 a point.

If you think the market is going to fall, you sell the index; if you think it is going to rise, you buy it. Say you wake up one morning and you hear something on the news which convinces you the market is going to fall. You decide to sell the index and bet £10 for each point that it drops. The market drops over the next couple of days to 1480 and you decide to close your bet. The bookies are quoting a price of 1478 to 1482. Your bet is closed at 1482, to show a profit of 16 points (the difference between 1498 and 1482), and you make £10 a point, so you pocket £160.

With City Index you can only keep your bet open for up to a month, with IG Index you can keep it open for as long as six months. City Index ask for a banker's reference, and once accepted you can bet on credit. IG Index ask for a deposit of 5 per cent of the value of the underlying contract. So if you bet £10 a point and the index stands at 1500 you pay the margin of £750 (5 per cent of 1500 times 10).

The taxman treats betting on the index as just that, and both bookmakers pay betting tax out of the spread between the buying and selling price of the index. You have no extra tax to pay.

HOW OPTIONS AND FUTURES ARE TAXED

Capital Gains Tax is the only tax you may ever have to pay on traded options and futures. With traded options your gain or loss is calculated using the difference between the traded option price when you bought your contract and when you sold it, just as if you were buying and selling shares.

With futures, your profit is calculated on the underlying value of the contract. The amount of margin you may have put up is ignored when you work out your gain or loss, whether it's options or futures.

Even if you do clean up in the options and futures market, remember your first slice of gains in any one tax year (£6,600 in 1987–88 tax year) is tax-free. And options and futures on Government stocks are entirely free of Capital Gains Tax, just as they are when you buy them directly.

MASTERING THE TECHNICALITIES

TRADED OPTIONS

On page 184 you can see a selection of traded options prices as they appeared in the *Financial Times* on 12 March 1987.

TRADED OPTIONS

Option		CALLS Apr.	CALLS Jly.	CALLS Oct.	PUTS Apr.	PUTS July	PUTS Oct.
Grand Met. (*490)	460	42	60	70	4	15	18
	500	20	37	48	25	30	37
	550	6	16	32	65	68	72
I.C.I. (*1318)	1250	100	145	165	15	32	50
	1300	67	110	135	34	50	750
	1350	42	85	110	60	75	100
	1400	22	65	90	930	105	120
	1450	13	45	70	135	140	155
Land Securities (*366)	330	39	45	56	1	6	9
	360	17	28	40	8	16	20
	390	6	13	24	27	34	38
Marks & Spen. (*237)	200	40	46	50	2	3	7
	220	22	29	36	4½	10	13
	240	9	17	25	13	18	23
Shell Trans. (*1177)	1000	178	178	202	6	15	20
	1050	128	145	163	8	23	38
	1100	83	102	127	22	37	47
	1150	42	62	90	45	55	70
Trafalgar House (*333)	280	57	64	76	2	3	7
	300	37	47	61	4	8	12
	330	17	29	41	15	20	25
	360	6	14	24	30	35	42

Let's take as our example Marks & Spencer. On that particular day Marks & Spencer's shares stood at 237p, as shown by the figure in brackets with the asterisk.

If you think the price of Marks & Spencer is about to rise you can choose from nine different call options. The one you choose will depend on how quickly you think Marks & Spencer's price will rise, how much money you want to commit to the option, and for how long.

Marks & Spencer has three different **exercise** or **strike prices**: 200, 220 and 240. These are the prices at which you have the right to buy or sell the underlying shares at the end of the option period.

Marks & Spencer's share price is less likely to fall below 200p than it is to rise above 240p. There is, therefore, less risk attached to the options with an exercise price of 200p than there is to those with an exercise price of 240p.

But it isn't just the exercise or striking price which varies. You can also choose from three different time scales. Each traded option is alloted a set of **expiry dates** which are set at three-monthly intervals throughout the year. In the case of Marks & Spencer they are January, April, July and October. But as you can see from the table there are only three expiry dates available at any one time. You stand a better chance of being right the longer your option has to run, which is why you pay more for your option.

If you hear the word **series** in connection with traded options, they are talking about options with the same exercise and expiry date. Thus the Marks & Spencer April 200 series is a reference to the options with an April expiry date and an exercise price of 200p. You will also hear them referred to as the Marks & Spencer April 200s. The term **class** refers to all the call options available on one share; the put options make up a separate class.

With traded options on the Stock Exchange, the traded option price is the same as the **premium** you pay. So in our example of Marks & Spencer, if you wanted to take out a call option at 200p with an April expiry date, the option premium is 40p a share. The minimum contract is normally an option on 1,000 shares. If you decided to take out the minimum of one contract, your option premium is £400 or 1,000 times 40p.

To illustrate how fast traded option prices can move in relation to the price of the underlying shares, and how it is also possible to make money out of falling markets, here is what happened to two Marks & Spencer option prices during those fateful few days between 31 March and 3 April 1987 when the FT-Actuaries Index fell 30 points on fears of a trade war with Japan.

Over that period Marks & Spencer's shares fell 11p from 220p to 209p. But if you had bought a put option with an exercise price of 220p and an April expiry date, it would have cost you 8p a share, or £80 for the minimum contract. Three days later that option rose to 15p, and you could have sold your minimum contract for £150, a profit of nearly 88 per cent.

However, if you had got it wrong and bought the matching call option it would have cost you 7p a share and three days later it would have been virtually worthless at between 3p and 4p.

Call options are referred to as being **in-the-money** when the exercise price is below the underlying share price. **At-the-money** options are those where the exercise price and the underlying share price are the same. **Out-of-the-money** call options – generally the most risky – are those where the exercise price is higher than the underlying shares. The reverse is the case for put options. Here in-the-money options are those where the exercise price is above the underlying share price, and so on.

Analysing trading options is a mathematician's delight. The beginner can start by understanding the difference between **intrinsic worth** and **time value**.

Only in-the-money options have any intrinsic worth. There is no mystique to intrinsic worth – it is simply the difference between the exercise price and the underlying share price. In our example of Marks & Spencer all the call options in the 200 series have an intrinsic worth of 37p which is 237p less 200p.

Time value is the option price stripped of its intrinsic worth. The longer the option has to run, the greater the time value. To return to Marks & Spencer's call options with an exercise price of 200p: the April option with not long to run has a time value of just 3p (the option price of 40p less the intrinsic value of 37p), the July option a time value of 9p (46p less 37p), and the October option with the longest to run has a time value of 13p (50p less 37p).

With Stock Exchange traded options you can't lose more than you have invested, which is not the case with futures contracts and some option contracts where you may be required to put up additional money as security if your investment goes bad on you.

You can exercise your traded option and buy the underlying shares at any time before the expiry date. But this isn't usually why investors buy traded options, and most contracts are sold in the market before they expire.

You can get started in traded options with rather less money than investing directly in shares. Always remember that when you invest in traded options you are speculating, and your aim is to make a lot of money, but you must be prepared to lose it all as well.

This being the case an investment of £250 in traded options is not too small. After all, if you double your money you won't resent paying your stockbroker's bill for minimum commission (it could be anything between £10 and £25). For larger deals you can expect to pay between 1 per cent and 2.5 per cent of the traded option premium plus between £1 and £1.50 per contract.

Be aware too that the traded option prices quoted in the newspapers aren't necessarily the prices at which you can deal. As with shares there is a spread between the price at which you can sell the options and the price at which you can buy them. Always ask your stockbroker for the price at which they are dealing for you.

If you have got this far, you have probably already acquired a stockbroker. Yours may not deal in traded options, or you may prefer to find a firm which specialises in these investments. The Options Development Group at The Stock Exchange produces a range of helpful leaflets on traded options including one containing the names of brokers who deal in traded options. Write to them at The Stock Exchange, London EC2N 1HP.

FUTURES

If, for example, you fancy a flutter on the dollar/pound exchange rate, you could take out a futures contract on the London International Financial Futures Exchange. On the day in question (12 March 1987) the dollar/pound exchange rate stood at 1.591 US dollars to the pound. If you think the pound will rise against the dollar you take out a call, if you think it will fall, you take out a put. The future for September delivery is quoted at 1.5665 dollars to the pound. This gives you the right to buy or sell £25,000 of sterling at an exchange rate of 1.5665 dollars to the pound when the contract is delivered in September. You think the dollar/pound exchange rate will rise so you take out a September call. Your initial investment or margin is $1,000 (£629) and the value of the underlying contract is $39,163.

Six weeks later the September option has risen to $1.6195 and you decide to take your profit and close your position. The underlying value of your contract is now worth £25,000 times 1.6195 – or $40,488 – so you make a profit of $1,325. But with the actual pound/dollar exchange rate now standing at 1.634, your profit is worth £811.

£££

14
Wealth by association

It really wasn't so very long ago that it was almost unheard of for women to make their own way in the world except as missionaries, nurses or governesses. Unless you inherited wealth, there was only one socially acceptable way for women to acquire money and that was via a man and marriage.

This is wealth by association and, like it or not, there is absolutely no doubt that money attracts money. But today's golddigger is in a much stronger bargaining position than her grandmother and she has far more weapons at her disposal.

○ You can go where money makes money. In the post Big Bang City there are now plenty of opportunities for women to storm the previously male-dominated world of foreign exchange, commodity and share dealing.

○ You can plug into the various women's networks designed to give women the contacts and confidence of the old boy network.

○ You can still marry wealth, or have wealthy friends. But this time use it to your advantage. If your husband is in business, use him as your training school. If you have a good idea and your husband has a good business brain, can you put the two together and start your own business.

○ You can also acquire the trappings. Looking right, flashing the right credit cards, having an answering machine – they may go against the grain, but they won't necessarily cost you a lot of money and there is no doubt that people judge by first impressions.

WHERE MONEY MAKES MONEY

Women are now taken much more seriously in the City. When the American banks came to London in their droves in the middle and late 1970s they brought with them women executives right up to the level of vice-president. It was this invasion of top-flight American women which gave British women the confidence to see that they too might one day have a place up there with the money makers, away from the typewriter and calculator.

Women were only allowed to become stockbrokers on the London Stock Exchange in 1973, although there was a woman stockbroker who managed to become a member of the now defunct Provincial Exchange as early as 1945. But there are still only 150 or so women stockbrokers out of a total membership of over 5,300. Even so, some of the City's top share experts are women.

Extel compile a yearly list of the top stockbrokers' analysts – the people who research the companies behind the shares. The list is compiled from votes taken among the City's leading institutions – the people on the receiving end of all that stockbroking advice. In 1986, 27 women appeared on the list, women like Judy Shaw at Greenwell Montagu (now at Morgan Grenfell) whose speciality is chemicals, Janet Sidaway at Scrimgeour Vickers who keeps an eye on the mechanical engineers, and Barbara Arzymanow also at Greenwell Montagu, who is the fount of all wisdom on health and household product companies.

Women are managing unit trusts. There is Jane Smith at Barrington; Sandra Stoker at County; Sarah Arkle, Caroline Phillips and Vanessa Donegan at Allied Dunbar. While at Legal &

General Michelle Barber's Far Eastern fund is currently up there among the top performers.

But women are still remarkable by their absence in merchant banking and very few have seen service up at the coal face during the merger mania of the last couple of years – when each successive takeover seemed larger and noisier than the last, and which saw companies as large as Distillers, British Home Stores, and Debenhams gobbled up by ambitious competitors.

One exception is Lesley Watts, who at the remarkably young age of 33 was the first woman corporate finance specialist to join the board of a City merchant bank.

Lesley Watts is a Cambridge law graduate. When she left university she worked on both sides of the Atlantic as a company lawyer with two leading firms of corporate lawyers. Her life as a merchant banker began when she joined Kleinwort Benson in 1981, since when her rise from the ranks to a seat on the board has been nothing short of meteoric.

It's been her job to help some of Britain's most acquisitive and aggressive entrepreneurs expand their businesses. One of her clients is Harry Solomon, whose food company Hillsdown Holdings has taken over some 70 companies since 1982, at least 14 of which involved takeover bids for quoted companies. Another is Alan Sugar of Amstrad, the man with a genius for marketing hi-fi and computers.

Lesley Watts doesn't think being a woman has been a disadvantage. *'In some ways it's been a plus. When I started there were so few women doing what I do that I couldn't fail to be noticed. I certainly never had any problem in the bank itself. I did sometimes feel that some of my clients felt they were being fobbed off with the B-team. But I think this was as much a function of my age as my sex. Occasionally it's been hard work convincing them that good advice doesn't only come from grey-haired men.'*

Round the clock trading is now a reality. If you are a big corporation and you want to buy Japanese yen at four o'clock in the morning, you can. Nowadays, when Tokyo closes, London takes over, and as London slows down, New York comes alive. It's an operation which requires an army of lean and hungry young turks, with nerves of steel, a flair for the market and a determination to outwit the competition. Trading, whether it's foreign exchange, commodities or financial futures, is a game of poker played over the telephone with the VDU as dice. And there are very few women doing it.

Whatever you have heard about trading in the City, believe every word of it and more. It's a world where streetwise cred gets you a lot further than the old school tie. It's where jackets come off at 7.30 in the morning, sleeves are rolled up 10 minutes later and ties are hanging loose by the time the first cup of coffee arrives. In other words it's very macho.

Dealers burn out fast – the average life of a dealer working under this sort of pressure is around 10 years – you're over the hill once you reach 35.

If you work for an American bank, your pay is related to how much money you make for your employer, and in good years top traders can expect to take home upwards of £250,000. But once you stop earning your keep, there is no place for sentiment. You are out on your ear.

The British banks don't pay so well but will always find a backroom career for their burnt-out traders.

Jill Harrison is one woman who has managed to penetrate this almost exclusively male preserve. She works for Chemical Bank, a big American bank. She had a spell on the dealing desk when she worked at another American bank.

Now in her early thirties she heads a team of specialists advising company treasurers on how to use the foreign exchange markets. She won't be drawn on how much she earns, except to say that her salary is partly dependent on how good she is. It's my guess that it's upwards of £50,000 a year. But then she does work long hours. Her normal working day begins at 7.30 in the morning and she rarely leaves her desk before 6.30 in the evening.

Jill Harrison got her first job in banking, like most of her generation, after leaving school with 'A' levels. She went to work for Hambros Bank, and her career in foreign exchange began when she threatened to leave the bank unless they gave her something more interesting to do other than count cheques. They found her a job in their foreign exchange dealing room. And she hasn't looked back.

Now the banks tend to recruit graduates rather than school leavers and salaries start at anything between £15,000 and

£25,000, and if you are any good you can expect to at least double your salary after three years. But you do have to be good, and not everyone manages to acquire a feel for the market.

You won't come across much sexual prejudice in the world of financial futures. The London International Financial Futures Market (LIFFE) only opened its doors in 1984, so it hasn't had time to become hide-bound by convention. There was also a shortage of trained traders in the early days, so much so that they were brought in from the United States and Australia. Many of them were women. Most have now returned home, but it does mean there has never been a time when the participation of women has ever looked anything but commonplace.

You would be forgiven for thinking that Stephanie Hanbury-Brown is an Australian. In fact she is English, but eight years ago she found herself working in Australia at a time when they were opening up their financial futures market. A friend answered a newspaper advertisement which simply asked for ambitious, go-ahead men and women. It turned out to be for the new financial futures market. Stephanie's friend got a job and encouraged her to apply too.

Stephanie's employers brought her back to Britain in 1982 when the London financial futures market opened here. It was at a time when most of the talent was imported and it was her job to go out and sell the idea of financial futures to the banks and other big City institutions.

She has recently been head-hunted by a leading US bank Morgan Guaranty, where she heads up the 20-strong financial futures operation as well as being in charge of the bank's US government bond department in London with a staff of 12 people. Salaries for jobs like this range between £60,000 and £90,000 a year, a figure which can easily be doubled with bonuses.

PLUG INTO THE NETWORKS

Hilary Sears is a City headhunter and a leading member of the City Women's Network. It was founded in 1978 by an American lawyer, Joni Nelson, who came to work in Britain. She was horrified to find how few British women were working in responsible positions in the City. She set about finding those that were, and the network started holding regular lunches.

Hilary Sears explains the thinking behind City Women's Network. *'It's the female answer to the old boy network. We aren't cocking a snook. But we do think it's important to realise how important these networks are. The old school tie, the gentleman's club – decisions are still influenced by these factors. We think women should have their own networks, where they can swap information, encourage each other, and find out where the jobs are.'*

Women who belong to the City Women's Network are already high achievers. Unless you are a professional of at least three years standing, you won't be accepted for membership. There are now around 200 members in fields as diverse as law, banking, medicine, journalism and public relations. They meet once a month for a formal lunch at one of the City livery halls. There are other meetings between lunches, and there is a monthly newsletter.

Ermine Evans is a member of the other main City-based network, Women in Banking. Ermine deals in Government stocks for one of the big clearing banks. She remembers a particularly rough patch when she was made to feel very unhappy by one of her male colleagues. *'I don't think it had anything to do with my sex. This particular person had a history of making people's lives difficult. But I still felt I was being victimised because I was a woman doing a job traditionally done by a man. It was paranoia, I know, but having other women to talk to helped a lot.'*

Women in Banking was formed in 1980 largely thanks to the initiative of women like Ann Watts at National Westminster and Tina Boyden at Barclays who head up the equal opportunities units in their respective banks. There are now 200 members, and a wide range of activities – anything from assertiveness training to informal lunches to meetings with speakers.

Nor are networks confined to the City. Network, for example, is an organisation for senior women with several branches outside London. Some networks have a long history. The Association of Women Solicitors came into existence in 1923, while the National Association of Women Pharmacists started its work in 1905.

If you like the idea of joining a network, find out if there is one in your industry, or you might prefer to join one of the more general organisations which take women from a wide range of occupations. It's up to you to find one you feel comfortable with.

The Women's National Commission was set up in 1967 to advise the Government on issues relating to women. The Commission publishes a directory of women's organisations, including most of the networks. You can get a copy from the Women's National Commission, Government Buildings, Great George Street, London SW1P 3AQ, tel: 01-270 5903.

HUSBAND AND WIFE TEAMS

The business world is full of husband and wife business teams, where the initial flair and feel for the market has come from the woman, and the business acumen is then provided by the man.

It's a cliché, but it seems that successful business marriages manage to combine the strengths of both sexes – female intuition with male ambition and drive. And in so doing create companies which challenge many long-held business beliefs about what makes a successful enterprise. They have a lot to teach much of the rest of British industry which stumbles on with too much head and not enough heart.

The message of all this is choose your husband with care! If you think you might one day have the makings of an entrepreneur, look for a husband – or find a business partner – who can complement your talents.

Laura Ashley is one of the manufacturing and retailing success stories of the last 20 years. Laura Ashley's tiny flower-sprigged designs first printed on her kitchen table spawned a multi-million pound enterprise with shops all over the world. It was Laura Ashley's love of her family, home and factory in Wales, and the people who worked in it, which set the tone of the whole enterprise. She still inspires a whole generation of home makers, and it's a tribute to her talent that the inspiration survived her death.

But if it hadn't been for Laura's husband, Bernard Ashley, Laura might have got no further than her kitchen table. It was Bernard's drive and enthusiasm which took his wife's ideas and splashed them across the world. Together they challenged the business convention that you can't be a successful manufacturer and retailer. It was the ideal business partnership, and there would be no chain of Laura Ashley shops today if the unique qualities of these two people hadn't come together.

It's a similar story at Body Shop, where the initial inspiration, and in this case entrepreneurial skill was provided by Anita Roddick. Her husband Thomas then joined her to help expand the business. Body Shop is another business to break out of the accepted mould. It is principally a manufacturing company. The company's public face, the high street chain of Body Shops, are for the main part franchised – a method of retailing still regarded with some suspicion in this country. But the Roddicks had the courage to see the potential for expanding the business fast, and giving the people who run the shops a real share in their success.

Women used to marry rich men for the meal ticket. Now they marry them for what they can teach them about business, and the more entrepreneurial the man, the more marriageable he is.

Jennifer D'Abo wouldn't put it quite like that, but she is the first to admit that she learned a lot from her years of marriage to Peter Cadbury, the colourful entrepreneur of West Television fame. Now a businesswoman in her own right, she has just sold the flourishing Rymans office equipment chain which was on its last legs when she bought it from the Burton Group.

GETTING THE TRAPPINGS RIGHT

Be honest, you do it, everyone does it. There can't be a person alive who doesn't make snap judgements about people based on those fateful first impressions. Of course first impressions often fade, and when it comes to your friends it's hard to remember what you first thought of them.

But in the world of money and business you don't get a second chance. It may not be your style, you may even think it is nothing short of deception, but if you want to clinch a deal, or get people to listen to you in a meeting, or give the appearance of efficiency, you must think about your image.

You may be living in a one-room flat, in the worst part of town, but no one need know if you have an answerphone, one smart set of clothes, and invest in taxis when you need to turn up to meetings in style.

If you earn enough, think about taking out a gold card. They are hard to justify on strictly financial grounds unless you need the automatic overdraft facility, but if you earn at least £20,000 a year they may be worth the investment if you need to project an aura of success.

FINALLY

Congratulations! You are now a fully-fledged Woman of Substance and you qualify to join that new breed of women who can stand alone both emotionally and financially if need be. Gone are all those feelings of financial inadequacy which left financial planning to fate.

You have seized control of your destiny – you no longer need to refer to anyone but yourself when faced with life's big financial decisions. Captain of your own ship, no one can sell you a bum product or give you bad advice – you know which savings plans are worth having and which advice is worth following. You know where you can expect to meet discrimination and how to fight it.

You are equipped to join the ranks of those who use their money to make money. This is the serious business of building wealth – the kind of wealth which leaves you free to lead the life you want, rather than the one imposed upon you by circumstance. The idea of starting your own business, or investing in stocks, shares and unit trusts, holds no fear for you. You know the risks and rewards and you are aware of your financial personality and which bits of it need working on.

But best of all, the scales have been lifted from your eyes and the fog has cleared. Women of Substance know that understanding money is the first step to enjoying it, and it's difficult to have the second without the first.

Useful addresses

The Agricultural Futures Exchange, Baltic Exchange Chambers, 24 St Mary Axe, London EC3P 8EP (01-283 5146)

Association of British Insurers, Aldermary House, Queen Street, London EC4N 1TT (01-248 4477)

Association of Futures Brokers and Dealers (AFBD), Plantation House, Mincing Lane, London EC3M 3DX (01-626 9763)

Banking Information Service, 10 Lombard Street, London EC3V 9AP (01-626 8486)

Banking Ombudsman, Citadel House, 5–11 Fetter Lane, London EC4A 1BR (01-583 1395)

British Franchise Association, Franchise Chambers, 75a Bell Street, Henley-on-Thames, Oxon RG9 2BD (0491-578049)

British Insurance Brokers' Association, BIBA House, 14 Bevis Marks, London EC3A 7NT (01-623 9043)

The Building Societies Association, 3 Savile Row, London W1X 1AF (01-437 0655)

City Index, Europe House, World Trade Centre, London E1 9AA (01-283 3667)

Company Pensions Information Centre, 7 Old Park Lane, London W1Y 3LJ (01-493 4757)

Consumers' Association, Castlemead, Gascoyne Way, Hertford, SG14 1SH (0992-589031)

Co-operative Development Agency (CDA), Broadmead House, 21 Panton Street, London SW1Y 4DR (01-839 2988)

Department of Employment's Small Firms Service, dial 100 and ask for Freephone Enterprise

Enterprise Agencies, c/o Business-in-the Community, 227a City Road, London EC1V 1LX (01-253 3716)

Equal Opportunities Commission, Overseas House, Quay Street, Manchester M3 3HN (061-833 9244)

Finance Houses Association, 18 Upper Grosvenor Street, London W1X 9PB (01-491 2783)

Financial Intermediaries, Managers and Brokers Regulatory Asssociation (FIMBRA), 22 Great Tower Street, London EC3R 5AQ (01-929 2711)

Homeloan Scheme, Department of the Environment, Room N21/21, 2 Marsham Street, London SW1P 3EB (01-212 3434)

IG Index, 9–11 Grosvenor Gardens, London SW1W 0BD (01-828 7233)

Insurance Brokers Registration Council, 15 St Helen's Place, London EC3A 6DS (01-588 4387)

Insurance Ombudsman Bureau, 31 Southampton Row, London WC1B 5HJ (01-242 8613)

Investment Management Regulatory Organisation (IMRO), Centrepoint, 103 New Oxford Street, London WC1A 1QH (01-379 7400)

Law Society, 113 Chancery Lane, London WC2A 1PL (01-242 1222)

Life Assurance and Unit Trust Regulatory Organisation (LAUTRO), Centrepoint, 103 New Oxford Street, London WC1A 1QH (01-379 7400)

London International Financial Futures Exchange (LIFFE), Royal Exchange, London EC3V 3PJ (01-623 0444)

The London Commodity Exchange, 1 Commodity Quay, St Katharine Dock, London E1 NAX (01-481 2080)

The London Metal Exchange, c/o Brian Reidy & Associates, Plantation House, Fenchurch Street, London EC3M 3AP (01-626 1828)

Money Management Magazine, Greystoke Place, Fetter Lane, London EC4A 1ND (01-405 6969)

National Association of Conveyancers, 2 Aspley Hill, Woburn Sands, Milton Keynes, MK17 8NJ (01-549 3636)

National Consumer Council, 20 Grosvenor Gardens, London SW1W 0DH (01-730 3469)

National Savings, General Enquiries (01-605 9477)

National Savings Bank, Cowglen, Glasgow G58 1SB (041-649 4555)

National Savings Certificates and SAYE Office, Milburngate House, Durham DH99 1NS (0385-64900 × 699)

National Savings Stock Register, Bond and Stock Office, Preston New Road, Marton, Blackpool, FY3 9YP (0253-66151)

Office of Fair Trading, Field House, 15–25 Breams Buildings, London EC4A 1PR (01-242 2858)

Planned Savings Magazine, 33–35 Bowling Green Lane, London EC1R 0DA (01-837 1212)

The Securities Association, Old Broad Street, London EC2N 1HP (01-588 2355)

The Securities and Investments Board (SIB), 3 Royal Exchange Buildings, London EC3V 3NL (01-283 2474)

The Stock Exchange, Old Broad Street, London EC2N 1HP (01-588 2355)

Unit Trust Association, Park House, 16 Finsbury Circus, London EC2M 7JP (01-638 3071)

Women in Enterprise, 26 Bond Street, Wakefield WF1 2QP (0924-361789)

Women's Enterprise Development Agency, Aston Science Park, Love Lane, Aston Triangle, Birmingham B7 4BJ (021-359 0981)

Women's National Commission, Government Offices, Great George Street, London SW1P 3AQ (01-270 5903)

Index